Legendary COMEDIES

Legendary COMEDIES

Peter Guttmacher

MetroBooks

MetroBooks

An Imprint of Friedman/Fairfax Publishers

© 1996 by Michael Friedman Publishing Group, Inc.

Library of Congress Cataloging-in-Publication data available upon request.

ISBN 1-56799-239-0

Editors: Stephen Slaybaugh and Carrie Smith
Art Director: Lynne Yeamans
Designer: Amanda Wilson
Photography Researcher: Darrell Perry
Photography Editor: Kathryn Culley

Color separations by Ocean Graphic International Company Ltd.
Printed in China by Leefung-Asco Printers Ltd.

For bulk purchases and special sales, please contact:
Friedman/Fairfax Publishers
Attention: Sales Department
15 West 26th Street
New York, NY 10010
212/685-6610   FAX 212/685-1307

Visit the Friedman/Fairfax Website:
http://www.webcom.com/friedman

Acknowledgments

The author wishes to acknowledge invaluable assistance from the headliners at the Academy of Motion Picture Arts and Sciences' Margaret Herrick research facilities.

CONTENTS

Due to the involuntary, simultaneous contraction of fifteen facial muscles, the upper lip is raised, partially uncovering the teeth and effecting a downward curving of the furrows that extend from the wings of both nostrils to the corners of the mouth. This produces a puffing out of the cheeks on the outer side of the furrows. Creases also occur under the eyes and may become permanent at the side edges of the eye. The eyes undergo reflex lacrimation and vascular engorgement. At the same time, an abrupt strong expiration of air is followed by spasmodic contractions of the chest and diaphragm, resulting in a series of expiration-inspiration microcycles with interval pauses. The whole body may be thrown backward, shaken or convulsed because of other spasmodic skeletal muscle contractions. We call this condition laughter.

—from the National Aeronautics and Space Administration's Enlightened Employee Health program

INTRODUCTION

Before we can properly examine the seminal nature of this elusive medium—which history has hitherto labeled Comedy, or Comedius Antiquitus, as the ancient Greeks once termed it—we must first delve minutely into the social milieu of the art form's historic roots in classical civilization. Marcus Antonius notes in his twenty-volume history of the Greco-Roman period that...scared you there for a second! But seriously folks, sneezing away the classical dust, we do know this: ever since those same ancient Greeks gave the smiley mask to one form of popular entertainment and the nasty mask to the other, friends, Romans, and countrymen alike have been flocking to theaters (movie and otherwise) for a few good belly laughs. After all, the word "comedy" comes from the Greek *komos*, referring to raucous revels in honor of the god Dionysus, inventor of wine making and in whose honor all those orgies were held. It's possible that these very hedonistic, gluttonous, drunken, and lascivious ceremonies first popularized the comedic form (and possibly college frat parties as well). And let's face it, since then, comedy has always been more popular than tragedy—perhaps because there has always been plenty of tragedy to go around in life.

Now, put down those grapes and put on your time-travel suits. Let's plow through about twenty-four hundred years of show biz history and watch each generation shamelessly steal bits, plots, gags, and characters from its predecessors, from amphitheater antics to medieval jesters and dumbshows to Goldoni's Commedia Dell'Arte's rough-and-tumble; from the Bard of Avon's Elizabethan/Jacobean playful wordiness to Molière's French social farce to Congreve's racy Restoration comedy of manners; from Lope de Vega's noble, zany Spanish panache to Lessing's German gems to Sheridan's eighteenth-century English return to naughtiness; from Gogol's restrained Russian roguery to Shaw and Wilde's rapier nineteenth-century wit and even to Grock's Swiss circus clowning. Humorous entertainment for the masses had distilled itself down to a powerful essence at the end of the 1800s—which just happened to coincide with the birth of the motion picture.

Baggy-panted vaudevillians, English music-hall mugs, and patter-speaking burlesque kings and queens were about to launch film comedy into the twentieth century. While film was still in its infancy, legendary stage performers were cutting their teeth in those smoky halls and getting ready to take the silver screen by storm in much the same way that the comedy clubs of the 1980s and 1990s have pipelined fresh faces into television and film.

That's where our journey begins: we'll track the twisty trail that comedy has carved from the famous footsteps of these silent giants right up to today's hipper-than-hip Hollywood household words. From madcap teams and screwball romances to no-holds-barred nutcases, and from stinging satires to contemporary cut-ups, we'll be time-tripping in and out of the laughs, lives, lines, and films of the funniest (and most humanly flawed) men and women to cop a closeup.

A disclaimer: while we sincerely hope that every film you find here will be one of your all-time favorites (or better yet, will become one), if there's a gem you can't find in our treasure trove or a star who didn't make the A-list, just remember what Groucho Marx told the young traveler who, looking for her Aunt Minne, knocked on the door of his overpopulated stateroom during *A Night at the Opera* (1935): "Well, you can come in and prowl around if you want to. If she isn't here, you could probably find someone just as good."

As has often been said, no one has ever died of laughter, which is good for these German women enjoying Charlie Chaplin's imitation of Hitler in The Great Dictator *(1940). The film was shown to some four hundred Berliners by the U.S. Military's Information Control Division on August 10, 1946. The picture was sprung by surprise on the Germans, who thought they were going to see* Kitty Foyle.

Chapter One

SILENT LAUGHTER SILENT TEARS

The films are, I think, victims of what may be a curious law.
Whenever an entirely new form is let loose upon the world,
it must begin at the very beginning.

—Walter Kerr, *The Silent Clowns*

He may not be dressed for the weather and his face may look frozen, but many people consider this humble individual the funniest film performer (and director) who ever lived. Ladies and gentlemen, the one and only Buster Keaton.

Great Beginnings in Humble Places

The roots of screen comedy can be traced most directly to the long tradition of the English city taverns, long the favorite place for sing-alongs that featured individual performers who joked as well as warbled. As this local entertainment grew into what became "music hall" performing, so did the stages that supported its acts. Drinks were still served on premises, but were found more often in a theater with a stage, seats for the patrons, and a bar in the back than in the smoky pubs of yester-year. When the Theater Regulation Act of 1843 prohibited drinking alcohol in legitimate theaters, nothing was said about boozing it up at the music-hall variety shows. Up went attendance. Up went comedy.

Meanwhile, across the Atlantic, minstrel shows, in their own folksy, racist way, were providing the same variety of thrills and laughs for mostly male stateside audiences. However, with the war of emancipation fought and won, and the idea slowly dawning that it may be of questionable taste for whites to rub their faces with burnt cork and caper around cretinously, the turn of the century saw a shift toward American refinement.

Vaudeville—named for the Vau de Vire valley in Normandy, France, where humorous, topical songs were popular—helped the variety show clean up its act. The second section of the minstrel show had traditionally been an olio, in which performers of all the lively arts (in blackface) had soloed one by one. Once the offensive material was eliminated and the sooty blackface was rubbed off, families flocked, and entrepreneurs raked in admissions. In these popular palaces of entertainment, for twenty cents you could catch any one of the continuous showings throughout the day and stay as long as you wanted.

By 1896, New York alone had seven vaudeville houses. By 1910, there were thirty-one, nurturing performers like W.C. Fields, Buster Keaton, Mae West, Will Rogers, and, later, Eddie Cantor, Jack Benny, Fred Allen, Milton Berle, George Burns and Gracie Allen, Bob Hope, and the Marx Brothers. Each act got approximately twenty minutes to strut its stuff during the show, with in-front-of-the-curtain comedians covering the concealed chaos backstage as another production number was being prepared. But comedy was far from mere time-filler. The cherished eighth spot on the bill, just before the big finale, was most often the domain of the jokester.

> **Slapstick is first and foremost, or at least is also, the dramatic expression of the tyranny of things.**
> —André Bazin

> **Non-anticipation on the part of the recipient of the pastry is the chief ingredient of the recipe.**
> —Mack Sennett

The Frenchman

The first film comedies were mostly one-reel adaptations of popular stage plays or vaudeville sketches, and they were usually a bit bumpy. Considering that early American cinema largely consisted of setting up a stationary camera before real events, we can hardly expect more. But inventor Thomas Edison was more interested in recording real Indian riders and firemen in his shorts than playing for laughs. And D.W. Griffith, who had his vision set on a grander dramatic scale, was known for his lack of humor, if anything. Still, little by little, fantastical funny men and women entered the new genre and made their presence as hilarious as their personal lives were often tragic.

As early as 1906, France's dapper, top-hatted, mustachioed comedian Max Linder had started injecting both imagination and a memorable character into a series of situation comedies whose roots were in boulevard farce. Writing, directing, and starring in short films like *Max Takes a Bath* (1910) and *Max Gets Married* (1910), he was soon a European sensation. His *Max Is Jealous* (1914) features Linder training his dog to guard his unfaithful spouse. The dog not only listens at her door for clandestine lovemaking but manages to telephone Linder at the office once it hears the hanky-panky. The result is a final frame of a dejected Max and pooch sharing a cozy breakfast—with the wife nowhere in sight. Max even kisses Fido as he goes out the door to work.

As funny as Linder's films were, his life was much less so. At the outbreak of World War I, he tried to enlist in the

ABOVE: "Way down upon the smarmy river": racist Americana from a minstrel show. RIGHT: A lean, mean, already legendary W.C. Fields does some huckstering in Two Flaming Youths (1927).

French army, but was rejected because of an old stomach injury and the chronic depression he suffered. Nevertheless, Linder put his film career on hold and delivered dispatches to the front in his own car during the war, only to be severely injured by an incoming shell. After war and convalescence, Linder ditched war-torn Paris and came to peaceful Hollywood. *Max Comes Across* (1917) features Max chasing—and being chased by—a rolling grand piano aboard an ocean liner on a stormy sea. *The Three Must-Get-Theres* (1922), a spoof of Douglas Fairbanks' *Three Musketeers* (1921), includes the enemies of D'Artagnan encircling him and advancing to skewer him at neck level, then stabbing one another when he ducks. Even with the physical comedy, the overall gentility of these films didn't mesh with the increasingly rough-and-tumble American taste in humor. The films flopped. Linder, now an outcast of the art form he had helped create, went home to Paris and killed himself.

Slapstick had already become comedy's (old) new wave. The name itself had come from the use in Italy's Commedia Dell' Arte and England's knockabout Punch and Judy puppet shows of a split stick that made a great "crack!" whenever it was slapped against someone. Surprisingly, director D.W. Griffith can perhaps take the credit for cranking out the blueprint upon which American slapstick screen comedies would be molded for decades to come.

The Curtain Pole (1908) features a fop who breaks a curtain pole while trying to help his sweetheart and valiantly goes out to get a replacement. On the way, he makes a pit stop into a saloon for a drink and emerges, plastered, with a pal to help him drive the new pole home in his buggy. The pole is so big that the drunken ride wreaks havoc through the entire town and a mob forms in pursuit of the oblivious fop. That fop was Mack Sennett, an Irish-Canadian actor who would give Hollywood comedy the kick in the pants it needed to get into high gear.

The King and His Fun Factory

Mikhal Sinnot was no dummy: acting was a lot more enjoyable than blacksmithing, which is what he had done in Quebec. So after Americanizing his moniker to Mack Sennett, the would-be actor drifted into Thomas Edison's Biograph Company in the early 1900s. At about the same time, the soon-to-be father of American film, D.W. Griffith, was making his own acting debut there. In 1909 alone, Sennett appeared in more than a hundred Biograph one-reelers, and as Griffith's directorial star rose, Sennett became a very enthusiastic acolyte, learning as much as he could about filmmaking.

In 1911, he had his first shot at it when the original director had a nervous breakdown. *Comrades* was a chase film with a scenario

Billy Bevan romances the princess of salami and sets fire to the ocean floor in Mack Sennett's A Sea Dog's Tale *(1926).*

> Words can hardly suggest how energetically they [the Keystone Kops] collided and bounced apart, meeting in full gallop around the corner of a house; how hard, how often they fell on their backsides; or with what fantastically adroit clumsiness they got themselves fouled up in folding ladders, garden hoses, tethered animals, and each other's headlong cross-purposes.
> —James Agee, on the Keystone Kops

"stolen" from the French Pathé Brothers films, and it was so energized and crazy that audiences loved it. With his flair for physical comedy, Sennett was soon directing all of Biograph's half-reel comedies, while the master concentrated on the one-reel dramas. After two years of apprenticeship, Sennett decided to go it alone .

In 1912, Sennett set up what he called his "fun factory," in Los Angeles, where Griffith himself had been doing winter filming since 1910—and he brought a wealth of comedic talent along for the ride. And what a ride it was: almost every major comedy star for the next twenty years would pass through Sennett's pie-in-the-face portal.

Of the more than five hundred Keystone comedies that Sennett produced, most fell somewhere in the middle of art, lunacy, and warfare. He claimed to have a direct phone line to the fire department, and at a moment's notice he could assemble cast and crew to whip up a sequence around local fires, demolition, auto races, parades, and other events.

> Once we stop to let anybody analyze us, we're sunk.
> —Mack Sennett

"It's got to move," was Sennett's famous saying, and his films did. Characters were clobbered with fists, feet, mallets, tire irons—anything handy—and even stopped when one would lose his weapon, genteelly allowing him to replace it before going back to knocking the hell out of one another. They might be bounced off telephone lines, shot through trees, or stretched to twice their length. Spontaneous, zany mayhem was king, and action was often improvised before the running camera in situations hazardous enough to make today's stuntmen faint; in one scene, a man was dangled over a cliff by a rope tied to the neck of a man in a car that was itself tilting on the precipice of the cliff!

Pratfalls, or Brodies (named for the famous Brooklyn Bridge leaper), were second nature and could be categorized into three types: the old-fashioned, which involved legs sliding out front and the bumper landing flat on his butt or his back; the stiff back, which was a dead fall from rocking back on the heels like a felled tree; and the 108, which often followed stepping on a banana peel and actually required a leap into the air and a backward fall, landing on the neck. Extras were also paid to take larger falls—at a salary of $2 per foot (30cm).

Chases were, of course, ubiquitous. Sennett even had a huge, revolving cyclorama built that flew scenery past any car or comedian. And if things ever calmed down a notch, you could usually count on funnyman Ford Sterling and the rest of the barreling, bumbling Kops to plunge themselves and their cars into the middle of the mayhem du jour to bring it back to a feverish pitch. The film that gives the most accurate feeling of the Keystone style is a publicity short called *The Hollywood Kid* (1924), which shows Sennett calmly sitting at a desk and listening to a writer's story pitch while all around whirl more explosions, chases, fights, and general chaos than is packed into most insurrections.

Even though the kindly Canadian started so many Hollywood comedians on the road to stardom, many felt ultimately constrained by Sennett's undiluted slapstick and the fast pace that could all but hide individual performances. Even as a star on the rise, Charlie Chaplin found that Sennett would cut his best bits of business when done in the middle of a room (where the action was), and so Chaplin learned to save them to accompany his entrances and exits. Little by little, Sennett's stars went on to bigger paychecks from bigger studios and to greater artistic control over their own material. Sennett himself had little interest as comedy calmed down to the screwball romances of the thirties and forties, but Hollywood never forgot his influence and energy and awarded him a special Oscar in 1937 for his lasting contribution to film comedy.

> *Say anything you like, but don't say I love to work. That sounds like Mary Pickford, the prissy bitch.*
> —Mabel Normand, proving her own point

The Tomboy

The one subject on which Sennett did deign to pause his camera was the movies' first real personality, comedienne, stuntwoman, and female director, Mabel Normand. The woman Charlie Chaplin referred to as "beauty among the beasts" during her Keystone days (she directed Chaplin in six films, more than anyone besides himself) was a star whose high jinx would make her the toast of Tinseltown—and later its shame.

Born in Boston in 1894 to a French pianist and an Irish lass and educated in a convent school, the young Mabel Fortescue got her start as a suc-

> *The most popular screen players are those who are loved for themselves, for their personalities. That is why you are so bitterly disappointed when you find that your favorite has faults just like the rest of humanity.*
> —Mabel Normand on fame

The glint in her eye was the real thing—vagabond Mabel Normand rides the rails in her first feature, Mickey *(1917)*.

cessful artist's and commercial model in New York by the age of fourteen, and went on to play small roles, both purely scenic as well as comedic, for the Biograph and later Vitagraph studios by age sixteen. The young woman so impressed Sennett (or Nappy, as she called him—a comment on his Napoleonic authority) that when he went to Hollywood to open his comedy studio for the New York Motion Picture Company, he offered Mabel $75 a week to become his leading lady. When she was rendered momentarily speechless at the offer, Mack and his money men interpreted her silence as a holdout: they upped the offer to $100. Again she was thunderstruck. They snorted and offered $125.

Mabel was well used for the money she was paid and spent six years with Sennett (who became her lover), sharpening her physical comedy and directing skills to a razor's edge and proving indispensable in front of the camera. As Chaplin once said of Keystone, "We used to go into a park with a stepladder, a bucket of whitewash, and Mabel Normand and make a picture." As a heroine, she was tied to railroad tracks, stuffed into sacks, flooded, and scorched, but the innocent-faced hoyden was game and gave as good as she got.

In one fight scene for an early Normand-Sennett film, the famed cross-eyed comic Ben Turpin was having trouble crossing his eyes, so Normand, in a fit of impatience, grabbed a pie from a nearby workman's lunch and threw it at Turpin's astonished face. The gag stuck, so to speak, and an act of brazenness became a classic gag. It was such brazenness that would be Mabel's boon and bane in times to come.

Enter the Fat Man

A gal as good as Mabel Normand needed a partner in crime. One day in early 1914, when Normand and Sennett were talking together at the top of the stairs outside Sennett's office at Keystone, a strange visitor waddled toward them. He was very fat and babyfaced, and was walking a yellow bull terrier. He announced to the dismayed couple that he was "the fat comic from the Long Beach stock company" and that he wanted to "get into the movies in the worst way." Sennett contemptuously dismissed Arbuckle, saying that fat men were too slow-moving to be effective in comedy. In answer, the man performed a series of backflips down the stairs, landed on his neck, and sprung to his feet smiling, unhurt, and

When his career reached its zenith in 1921, he was signed to a deal that no other comedian, not even Charlie Chaplin, had achieved—having complete control in every aspect of film from direction to casting as well as starring in his own feature-length comedies. His salary was one million dollars per year at the time when the average Los Angeles home cost two thousand dollars and the average income was something near six dollars per week. In 1921 Roscoe Conklin Arbuckle was among the wealthiest, most popular, most loved movie comedians in the world. And in 1921 he also became the most hated.
—Andy Edmonds, Frame Up! The Untold Story of Roscoe "Fatty" Arbuckle

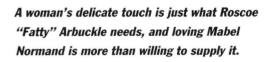

A woman's delicate touch is just what Roscoe "Fatty" Arbuckle needs, and loving Mabel Normand is more than willing to supply it.

unwinded. "Fatty," the astounded Sennett said, "you're in the movies."

Weighing fourteen pounds (6.4kg) at birth in 1887, Roscoe "Fatty" Arbuckle was the son of a Kansas fundamentalist mother and a whiskey-soaked father whose family moved to Santa Ana, California, when his father abandoned them. A second-grade dropout, Arbuckle had done a stint as a boy singer in San Francisco and had gone into vaudeville by the age of thirteen. He was primed and ready to go.

Sennett unleashed the three-hundred-pound (136kg) Fatty on the screen world in *The Knockout* (1914), in which Arbuckle, in too-short trousers, too-tight jacket, and too-teeny bowler, defends Normand's honor by boxing everybody in sight, then motions for the camera to tilt up to give him privacy while he changes

THE CLOWNS DON'T GET ALL THE FUNNY LINES

Samuel Goldwyn—native of Warsaw, Poland; ex–glovemaker; and legendary, paternal Hollywood producer of unsur- passed family entertainment—was also a star in his own right. His Goldwynisms became almost as famous as the films—like Squaw Man *(1913),* Wuthering Heights *(1939), and* The Best Years of Our Lives *(1946)—he produced. No one could mangle syntax or malaprop like Uncle Sam. Here are just a few of his diamonds in the rough. Imagine keep- ing a straight face while in a meeting with him...*

"Gentlemen—include me out!"

"Let's bring it up to date with some snappy nineteenth- century dialogue."

"A verbal contract isn't worth the paper it's printed on."

"Louella Parsons is stronger than Samson. He needed two columns to bring the house down. Louella can do it in one."

"I would be sticking my head in a moose."

"I'll give you a definite maybe."

"Let's have some new clichés."

"You should be goddamned proud, kid—you should never do another thing in your life." (To André Previn on his score for Porgy and Bess *[1959])*

"If Roosevelt were alive, he'd turn in his grave."

"Tell me, how do you love the picture?" (To a member of a preview audience)

"It's more than magnificent—it's mediocre."

"We have all passed a lot of water since then."

"In this business, it's dog eat dog, and nobody's going to eat me."

"Yes, I'm going to have a bust made of them." (Responding to a compliment on his wife's hands)

"You just don't realize what life is all about until you have found yourself lying on the brink of a great abscess."

"A producer shouldn't get ulcers, he should give them."

"You've got to take the bull by the teeth."

"I don't care if it doesn't make a nickel. I just want every man, woman, and child in America to see it." (On The Best Years of Our Lives*)*

"It's spreading like wildflowers."

"Anyone who goes to a psychiatrist should have his head examined."

"The trouble with this business is the dearth of bad pictures."

"First you have a good story, then a good treatment, and next a first-rate director. After that, you hire a competent cast and even then, you have only the mucus of a good picture."

"I can answer you in two words. Im Possible!"

into his boxing trunks. In *Miss Fatty's Seaside Lovers* (1915) he dressed in drag and was dropped from an airplane. In *His Wife's Mistake* (1916) he was agile enough to waltz with a revolving door. Master food fighter, somersault expert—the fat man could do it all with demented dexterity, and when teamed up with the equally innocent-looking yet loopy Normand, he became very hot, very quickly.

Pictures such as *Fatty and Mabel Adrift* (1915)—in which the love-smitten farmhand, Fatty, playfully squirts his lady love with an udder full of real milk and then gets so distracted that he almost milks a horse—tickled millions. Sennett's film also included a scene in which Fatty and Mabel's house is washed out to sea while they sleep. Their wake-up scene the next morning is priceless.

Arbuckle, on the other hand, had a price. By 1916, his popular- ity was so great and his interest in directing his own material was growing so strong that he left Sennett for greener pastures, a mil- lion-dollar, multiyear contract with Paramount, and his own pri- vate production company, called Comique. After Arbuckle's departure, Normand was likewise lured away; with the success of Sennett's first feature, *Mickey* (1917), she was temporarily stolen away by Samuel Goldwyn's unprecedented offer of $3,500 a week— the highest salary a film actor had ever commanded.

Successful as they both were, Fatty and Mabel would each take that long, dark slide down from the firmament to scandal and death. In 1921, Arbuckle was tried for the rape with a champagne bottle of starlet Virginia Rappe and her subsequent death from peritonitis. Though found innocent, he would be banned from Hollywood for life by the Hays Office (President Warren G. Harding had appointed former Postmaster General Will Hays to police morality in Tinseltown). Later directing sequences for his friend Buster Keaton under the pseudonym Will B. Goode, Arbuckle wasn't rehired to act until twelve years after his humiliation. Filming two shorts in the sizzling heat of a Brooklyn summer, Fatty concluded his first film by saying, "This is the happiest day of my life." The next morning, he was found dead in his hotel room from a heart attack.

Mabel's notoriously wild ways led her to scandal, as well. During a fight with Goldwyn vice president Abraham Lehr over another actress getting cast in a picture she wanted, Normand backed the executive into a corner, sprayed her perfume all over him, and later told his wife in passing that she had seen him coming out of a high-priced bordello. After being set to wed Sennett in 1915, she discovered him sleeping with starlet Mae Busch on the eve of their wedding. In the subsequent melee, Busch clobbered Normand over the head with a vase, fracturing her skull and causing her to go into a coma.

That was kid stuff. When her cocaine addiction became public knowledge, Mabel was soon box-office poison. She became the prime suspect in the sensational murder of playboy William Desmond Taylor, and her own chauffeur shot another of her lovers, the son of a Texas oil millionaire. In 1930, at the ripe old age of thirty-six, her fast life ended because of tuberculosis and pneumonia. Mabel and Fatty proved that just because it's a comedy doesn't mean that it has a happy ending.

That Amazing Little Fellow

The same year that Fatty Arbuckle came to Keystone to be amply packaged as a star, a young English music-hall clown made the trip west and began a career rise that would make him the most famous performer of his or any other time, changing comedy forever. Although he started in film slapstick (and in a donated pair of Fatty Arbuckle's trousers for his first incarnation of his tramp character), Charles Spencer Chaplin quickly learned that the screen chaos Sennett was famous for had to be motivated in order for the audience to connect with any character, and including the audience on a conspiratorial level was an even surer way to their

hearts and wallets. Maybe most important, he realized that great comedy was always played seriously. Egomaniacal? Perhaps. Sentimental? At times. But Chaplin was the acknowledged genius of silent laughter and pathos.

Charlie Chaplin's boyhood, however, contained nothing to laugh about. One of two young sons of a music-hall comic singer and a soubrette, he grew up in London's slums until his father's death from alcoholism, after which poverty and malnutrition drove his mother to a mental breakdown. After she was committed to an institution, Charlie and his brother, Sydney, were placed in a rather Dickensian workhouse called Lambeth until their mother's release. The reunited family, which later moved to odiferous lodgings between a slaughterhouse and a pickle factory, was so poor that the brothers shared one pair of shoes between them.

At the tender age of nine, Charlie hit the boards, joining a clog dancing and pantomime troupe called the Lancashire Lads at Manchester's Theatre Royal. After a few years with the lads, he took odd jobs as a naval shop errand boy, a newsboy, a printer's helper, and a glassblower before finally landing the part of Bill, the messenger boy, in a three-year touring production of William Gillette's *Sherlock Holmes*. By 1908, big brother Sydney had brought Charlie into top London music-hall impresario Fred Karno's troupe, the Mumming Birds, for a stint at Paris' famed Folies-Bergères. When the Karno company traveled to New York City in 1910, Charlie went with them and toured the states for two years. During the next trip to America, in *A Night in an English Music Hall* (1912), Chaplin developed the choice role of "the inebriate" in the audience, who gave a hilarious running commentary throughout the entire show. Mack Sennett and Mabel Normand caught his act in Philadelphia and telegraphed the theater with the question "Is there a man named Chafin in your company, or something like that?"

In 1914, comedy's first feature, Tillie's Punctured Romance, featured no less than Mabel Normand, Marie Dressler, Charlie Chase, Chester Conklin, Mack Swain, Minta Durfee, the Keystone Kops, and the Little Tramp himself.

ABOVE: *Filet of sole, anyone? Chaplin relishes one of his most famous comic scenes in* The Gold Rush *(1924).* BELOW: *A little man (Charlie Chaplin) with a big heart for a blind flower seller (Virginia Cherrill) in perhaps his finest film,* City Lights *(1931).*

Sennett offered Chaplin three times his tour salary, or $150 a week, to work for his starting studio making two-reelers, which were shot at a rate of one every two or three days. In his screen debut, *Making a Living* (1913), Chaplin gleefully threw himself into the knockabout scenes, kicking, falling, and flailing with the best of them, though he had other things in mind. In *Mabel's Married Life* (1914), Chaplin was already giving an early glimpse of just

how funny seriousness could be. In one of the most hilarious scenes of the movie, as he has a lengthy, nuanced, volatile, and completely believable drunken discussion with the tailor's dummy he mistakes for a rival for Miss Normand's love.

By 1914, when Sennett and Normand's—and comedy's—first feature, *Tillie's Punctured Romance*, hit the big screen, Chaplin was already a rising star with a shabby coat, oversize pants, a bowler, a cane, and a little mustache. So, in 1915, after making thirty-five films for Sennett in two years—as Arbuckle would a year later—Chaplin went to the greener pastures of Chicago's Essanay Film Company. A salary of $1,250 a week for fourteen films a year was a steep one, and at the contract signing in Chicago's Alexandra Hotel, Essanay officials got cold feet and questioned Chaplin's popularity. As in a bit from one of his films, Chaplin's answer to their worries was to secretly engage a hotel messenger to walk around the lobby, loudly paging him. When the money men saw the huge crowd that gathered at the mere mention of Chaplin's name, they had no recourse but to sign on the dotted line.

At Essanay, Chaplin's tramp character gelled even further in *The Tramp* (1915), and he began to explore just how seriously an audience could take him while laughing at him in the same film. In *The Police* (1915), the tramp is a released criminal who has tried to go straight, during which time he is mugged and not only goes through his own pockets looking for valuables to fork over, but impulsively goes through his assailant's pockets as well. When, in the same film, the tramp is later caught robbing the home of a beautiful, sympathetic woman (Chaplin's leading lady of thirty-four films, Edna Purviance), he goes along with her story that he is her husband.

Immediately after the police's exit, he begins acting exactly as her husband does and is perfect at it.

Chaplin and his fans were discovering together that this tramp could do anything and manipulate everything, and yet was always sadly a little outside of life. As audiences would later see, this outsider could model classic Greek poses as well as any Olympian, if it meant evading spa authorities—as in *The Cure* (1916). If it pleased him, he could roller skate while performing an interpretive dance, as in *The Rink* (1916). He could be the dashing Don José, managing his saber to play billiards with scallions when he wanted to woo a fair maiden, as in *Carmen* (1916). He could be more convincingly seasick than any actor should ever want to be, as in *The Immigrant* (1917). He could appear as tragically fatherly as he is childlike, as in *The Kid* (1920). He could mush sled dogs in Alaska (with cornflakes used to imitate snow) like a pro and make a shoe appear delectable (well, it was licorice) when he was hungry enough, as in *The Gold Rush* (1924).

The comic everyman's rise was meteoric. After a year at Essanay, the twenty-seven-year-old Chaplin went to Mutual Pictures in 1916 to make twelve films in a year, at $10,000 a week. (After the signing, Chaplin took a train trip to visit New York, and when word leaked of his travel, crowds mobbed the stations at virtually every stop, demanding an appearance as they would of a U.S. president.) After only a year, Mutual offered him an annual salary of $1 million—his salary had multiplied 384 times itself in the five years since his first movie contract—to stay, but Chaplin chose to establish his own studio. Two years later, he joined forces with giants D.W. Griffith, Douglas Fairbanks, and Mary Pickford to create the model for all independent film companies to come, United Artists.

ALL THINGS TO ALL PEOPLE

A lot of people have said a lot of things about the genius and temperament of Charlie Chaplin. With talent and ego that were the size of some small countries, it's only natural that people had sizable things to say about him. Here are a few of the choicest comments...both Charlie's and his, ahem, admirers.

"I remain just one thing and one thing only, and that is a clown. It places me on a far higher plane than any politician."
　　—Charlie Chaplin

"The son of a bitch is a ballet dancer! He's the best ballet dancer that ever lived, and if I get a good chance I'll strangle him with my bare hands."
　　—W. C. Fields, comedian

"Chaplin is the only man in the world I want to meet."
　　—Vladimir Lenin, Russian revolutionary leader

"[Chaplin is] one of the worst appreciators of comedy outside himself and his own genius."
　　—James Thurber, writer and cartoonist

"It is impossible to satirize Hitler, but Chaplin came closer than any other artist in getting to the reality, the bone beneath the skin."
　　—Albert Speer, Hitler's architect

"For me they are the most beautiful films in the world.... Chaplin means more to me than the idea of God."
　　—François Truffaut, director

"If people don't sit at Chaplin's feet, he goes out and stands where they're sitting."
　　—Herman J. Mankiewicz, producer

"It's easy for you—all this pantomime!"
　　—Harpo Marx, famous mime, after emerging with Chaplin from a showing of City Lights *(1931)*

"[Chaplin is an] obstinate, suspicious, egocentric, maddening, and lovable genius of a problem child."
　　—Mary Pickford, actress

"[Chaplin has the] power to stand for a sort of concentrated essence of the common man, for the ineradicable belief in decency that exists in the hearts of ordinary people, at any rate, in the West."
　　—George Orwell, author and visionary

"When he found a voice to say what was on his mind, he was like a child of eight writing lyrics for Beethoven's Ninth."
　　—Billy Wilder, director

"The only one of us who listened and accepted the role of genius [that] intellectual critics thrust upon him was Chaplin. Sometimes, I suspect that much of the trouble he's been in started the first time he had read that he was a sublime artist and a first-rate artist. He believed every word of it and tried to live and think accordingly."
　　—Buster Keaton, comedian

A Holdout in Modern Times

When they first formed United Artists, Chaplin and Fairbanks often acted as friendly sounding-boards for each other's ideas as they took long walks around Hollywood, during which they would occasionally be mobbed by fans. Since no audience had ever heard them speak, the pair sometimes entertained themselves by talking in squeaky, high-pitched voices just to astonish their admirers.

Yet speaking was no laughing matter. Times were changing. With the success of Al Jolson's *The Jazz Singer* (1927), the talkies were an inevitability. Chaplin didn't agree. His maudlin masterpiece of mirth *City Lights* (1931) had been resolutely silent except for a gabble of unintelligible voices and a swallowed whistle, and it had made $400,000 in its first twelve weeks—a box-office first. Still, he knew that he would have to talk sometime. The problem wasn't a squeaky voice, but rather that when he did speak, the cultured Englishman would sound very little like the Little Tramp.

Chaplin's farewell to the silents and to the tramp was also one of his very best films. The inspiration for *Modern Times* (1936) had come to him while having a $1.50 lunch with a near-indigent friend—a victim of the Great Depression—

who was railing against the mechanization of the modern world. Spying the conveyor belt—rather than busboys—that whisked the L.A. diners' plates into the kitchen, the friend exclaimed with disgust, "That's what I mean! Belts! Machines! We are even becoming machines!" After Chaplin hazily concurred, his friend got up not to flee in frustration but to say, "All right, Charlie! I'll meet you here tomorrow and we'll groan over it some more." Chaplin later remembered thinking to himself, "I see it better. He hates it, he revolts against mechanization, but he won't or can't escape it. Blithely, without recognizing its inescapability, he promises to come back, tomorrow. Charming."

Contrary to his Keystone pace of old, Chaplin had made only four movies during the past decade, but each had been a smash. He planned no less for his silent swansong. Production number five (Chaplin had become increasingly secretive about his films and never titled them until completed) was under way. It would become a story about an assembly-line worker (the tramp) at the Electro Steel Corporation...who goes crazy from the pressure and from being sucked into the gears of a machine, and disrupts the entire factory...is institutionalized in an asylum...rehabilitated, released, and almost immediately and hilariously mistaken for a communist agitator...institutionalized in prison...mistakenly fed cocaine with his prison gruel...energized to defeat a prison break...released reluctantly once again into society...where he hilariously tries to get rearrested...fantastically fails at a series of jobs—a roller-skating nightwatchman, assistant to a machinist (the Sennett regular, Chester Conklin), and finally a singing waiter who sings expert

ABOVE: Adenoid Hynkel of Tomania (Chaplin) flanked by Herr Garbitch (Cedric Hardwicke, at left) and Benzino Napaloni of Bacteria (Jack Oakie) in the controversial lampoon of Hitler, The Great Dictator (1940). RIGHT: The god Pan? No, it's just Chaplin after a little too much time on the assembly line in Modern Times (1936).

gibberish...and meets the gamin, a homeless girl on the lam with whom he tries to put down roots and who comes to share his wayward, exiled existence.

The highlights of *Modern Times* are the factory scenes—with the crazed Chaplin, wielding his two twitching wrenches, becoming the Panlike god of compulsive nut-tightening—which are almost as funny as Chaplin's reaction to the nose candy inadvertently dumped on his prison food. And in his own bit of machine bashing, there is an unforgettable sequence in which the tramp is serviced by the timesaving Biddows Feeding Machine (explained in sound on a phonograph record) while he's still on the assembly line. Naturally, the machine goes haywire, and each course becomes a new nightmare for the obliging but panicked worker—though his mouth is daintily wiped by a mechanical napkin after every disaster. The corn bit would have been enough to send Max Sennett helpless to the floor. As Harry Evans colorfully described it in his review at the time in *Family Circle* magazine, "The ear of corn comes up with all the gentleness of Joe Louis's left hook, smacks Charlie in the pan, starts revolving like a buzz saw, and gives his entire face a thorough corn-and-butter massage."

It was a fine send-off to Hollywood's silent age. Chaplin would, of course, go on to conquer the talkies in his next picture, *The Great Dictator* (1940), but despite being lauded throughout his life for his incredible ability to communicate poetically and comically, criminal charges ranging from tax evasion to communist leanings to a paternity suit would brand him as "an undesirable alien" and force him from the United States in 1952. An embittered Chaplin would have this to say in reply: "I have no further use for America. I wouldn't go back there if Jesus Christ was President!" So began the twenty-year exile of America's most beloved actor.

Buster Keaton: The Great Stone Face

In Fatty Arbuckle's first independent production, *Butcher Boy* (1917), a strangely riveting, moon-eyed, somber, soulful, almost otherworldly presence makes himself known. It is Buster Keaton in his first film appearance, and an impromptu one at that. A longtime vaudeville headliner, he was in New York, killing time before rehearsals for the Broadway play *The Passing Show of 1917* were to begin, when a pal invited him down to Comique, Arbuckle's new studio. The congenial Fatty quickly recognized Keaton from the stage and invited him to take a part in the film he was doing. Keaton could play a general-store customer who, after buying a twenty-five-cent pail of molasses, inadvertently puts his payment in the goo and, with Arbuckle and his bug-eyed nephew, Al Saint John, subsequently tries to retrieve it. Buster was excited to play the part, but—future director that he was—he wanted to explore something else first. Keaton later recalled, "The first thing I did was make a friend with

the cameraman and get in the cutting room and tear a camera to pieces [to] find out things I could do with that camera that I couldn't do on stage."

Satisfied with his exploration and having perused the previous day's rushes, Keaton was ready on the set the following day and executed his sticky gag so well that he later boasted that the bit in *Butcher Boy* "was the only movie comedy scene made with a newcomer that was photographed only once": he nailed it on the first take. He had also nailed a fast friendship

The bearded homunculus at the bottom was billed as "the human mop" when he headlined with his ma and pa as The Three Keatons.

with Arbuckle and a fascination with the possibilities of film. He stayed on at the studio for a salary equal to one-sixth of what he was to make on Broadway, and after fifteen other films with Fatty, Keaton was on his way to becoming one of the most visionary directors of all time, a stuntman with few equals, and an actor whose soulful, melancholic indestructibility would be the only rival to Chaplin's heartfelt, playful, inventive tramp.

Buster had traveled a long way to that fateful day at Comique. Born during a cyclone near his parents' medicine show in Piqua, Kansas, on October 4, 1895, Joseph Francis Keaton, Jr., was soon part of the act. As Joseph Senior recalled, "My wife had given birth to a son—our first baby. I was awfully glad. I could see the time coming, when the little feller got some older, when I wouldn't have to play the bloodhound in *Uncle Tom's Cabin*."

At six months of age, Joe Junior took a tumble down a flight of hotel lobby steps, and the elder Keaton's business partner—one Harry Houdini—amazedly picked up the unfazed, tearless tyke and said, "That's some buster your baby took." The name stuck. A bizarrely bewigged and bearded Buster turned out to be a veritable human prop for his parents' act, The Three Keatons. "My wife and I threw Buster about the stage like a medicine ball," Keaton

all he could from his unstintingly generous mentor. Upon his return from an eleven-month military stint during World War I, Keaton was offered a $1,000-a-week contract by Warner Brothers to star in their films; instead, he chose $250 a week to stay with Fatty and hone his craft.

Keaton also began to lobby for filmic reality. In *Desert Hero* (1919), in which Fatty was to be thrown from a moving train and roll down a steep embankment, across a dusty street, and in through the doors of a saloon, Keaton suggested they do it for real—in one take. He had calculated the physics, and it was possible. Arbuckle demurred, so Keaton padded himself out and hopped into Fatty's costume, performing the feat flawlessly. Throughout his career, he would do incredible stunts for other actors, just to show that the stunts could be done.

By the time Arbuckle left the two-reeler world of Comique to do features, Buster was left in the driver's seat and was ready to roll. His first independent film, *One Week* (1920), was already more imaginative and stylistically advanced than any film of its time. In it, two newlyweds inherit a prefab house and put it together so poorly that it hardly resembles

*ABOVE: Keaton is a projectionist who gets "wrapped up in his work" in perhaps his most visionary comedy, **Sherlock Jr.** (1924). BELOW: Keaton almost drowned filming this incredible climactic sequence from **Our Hospitality** (1923). The two minutes that follow this shot are even hairier.*

Senior admitted. Before Buster was through with the family act, he knew how to take every imaginable fall in acts billing him, among other things, as "the human mop"— for which his father grasped him by the feet and swabbed the floor with his head.

As well as learning to protect himself, Buster also learned that straight-faced was the way to play it. When, as a tyke, he was thrown by his father into an overturned bass drum, Buster jumped out smiling to show he was unhurt. No laughs. The next time he came out deadpan. Big laughs. From then on, if he cracked a smile, the old man would hiss, "Face, face!" or gave him a real wallop during the next bit. As Keaton remembered, "He kept after me, never let up, and in a few years it was automatic. Then when I'd step on a stage or in front of a camera, I couldn't smile." What critics would in time call "The Great Stone Face" was set.

Obsessed from adolescence with gadgetry and physics, the veteran vaudevillian was primed for film when opportunity knocked. At Comique, Keaton became Arbuckle's right-hand man, assistant director, and screen sidekick, content to yield the limelight and learn

> *No other comedian could do so much with a deadpan. He used this great, sad, motionless face to suggest various related things: a one-track mind near the track's end of pure insanity; mulish imperturbability under the wildest of circumstances; an awe-inspiring sort of patience and power to survive, proper to granite but uncanny to flesh and blood. Everything that he was and did bore out this rigid face and played laughs against it.*
> —writer James Agee, on Buster Keaton

That next step is going to be a doozy for Buster, the dude-turned-riverboatman in **Steamboat Bill Jr. (1927).**

a house at all. The inside is little better—what can you do with an oven on the ceiling? During a housewarming that is plagued by a windstorm, the house goes up on one corner and begins to spin, hurling guests and hosts out of every window and door. When Buster tries to reenter the spinning domicile, he miscalculates his dives at the front door and repeatedly smashes into the side of the house until a perfectly planned dive gets him in, tumbles him through every room in the house, and spits him out again. And as if this isn't bad enough, Keaton's final attempt to tow his entire house across the railroad track from the wrong lot to where it should be yields one of the wildest and most ironic endings that has ever graced a silent film. This film and others like it would lead critics to call Keaton a surrealist even before surrealism existed.

The surrealist was a perfectionist when it came to gags. In *The Boat* (1921), he wanted a bit in which a newly built ship, with himself aboard, slides down a chute into the water—and straight to the bottom. But a big boat, even one with ample holes, won't sink any way but slowly. So Buster loaded it with sixteen hundred pounds (726kg) of pig iron and track ties. Still no soap. A breakaway stern? Float it did. More holes in the bow? The wood is just too buoyant. Finally, $60,000 later, the patient Keaton connects a cable to the stern with an immense anchor at its belly and the end towed by an off-camera tugboat. The result is said to have caused the longest laugh in movie history.

Indeed, Keaton the director and film editor was endlessly inventive from film to film, and as an actor he endlessly risked his life in stunts that would today be achieved through trick photography. In *Sherlock Jr.* (1924), it's incredible enough that he rides a motorcycle at top speed across an aqueduct that sports a twenty-foot (6m) gap—riding across the tops of two trucks that happen to be speeding through the opening—only to have the entire 15-foot (4.6m)-high structure collapse mere seconds after he rides off the other side. Later, he is sitting on the front handlebars of a speeding motorcycle when the driver is bumped off. As writer James Agee noted, Keaton "whips through city traffic, breaks up a tug-of-war, gets a shovelful of dirt in the face from each of a long line of Rockette-timed ditch diggers, approaches a log at high speed, which is hinged open by dynamite precisely soon enough to let him through, and, hitting an obstruction, leaves the handlebars like an arrow leaving a bow, whams through the window of a shack in which the heroine is about to be violated, and hits the villain feet-first, knocking him through the opposite wall."

Keaton actually broke his neck in a railroad-car jump in that picture and didn't even know it (save the occasional blinding headache) until doctors pointed out the healed fracture to him in an X-ray years later. Keaton also nearly died for his art. In *Our Hospitality* (1923), the camera records him being washed down rapids when his cable snaps, and again he almost drowns when he finds himself suspended a little too close to a waterfall. He dived off an eight-foot-five-inch (2.6m)-high suspension bridge in *Paleface* (1921) and from an ocean liner in *The Navigator* (1924). He dived fifty feet (15.2m) into a pool, only to miss it and crash through fake pavement in *Hard Luck* (1921), a stunt that sustained him a great number of cuts and bruises. Perhaps genius is pain.

Yep, that cannonball ought to be coming out any minute in Keaton's personal favorite, The General *(1927).*

Neck bones aside, Keaton constantly broke new conceptual ground. In *Sherlock Jr.*, Keaton the projectionist somberly walks into the film he is showing, and when the film's cast tires of him, he finds himself transported seamlessly to a crowded city street...then to the edge of a cliff...to a lion-infested jungle...to the desert...and finally to that near-fatal locomotive. He liked to brag: "Every cameraman in the business went to see that picture more than once, trying to figure out how the hell we did it."

He may have almost never used a double, but in *The Playhouse* (1921), Keaton took the trick of double exposure where no film had gone before. He didn't just create a scene containing two versions of himself. He created a concert hall in which every member of the orchestra, the audience in the boxes, the ticket sellers, and even the ticket buyers were all him. You can imagine the credits.

Buster's stoic screen persona took every blow that life dealt him. However, at the end of the riverboat romance *Steamboat Bill Jr.* (1927), he created the blow to end all blows. On location near the Sacramento River, $100,000 worth of street sets were altered for an additional $35,000 so that a cyclone could blow them to pieces—courtesy of a 120-foot (36.6m) crane and a few wind machines.

The sequence, starting from when the hospital that houses Buster blows away around him, is astounding. Tree trunks and debris fly through the air like flocks of birds. A car hood goes sailing down the street, with its owner sailing after it. Keaton seems to defy gravity as he tries to walk against the wind's force. The final moment—one of the most famous in film history—in which the two-thousand-pound (907kg) side of a house falls on him and he emerges unharmed, as the opening for the attic window passes

right over him, is a marvel of moviemaking. There were exactly three inches (7.6cm) of clearance past his head and over each shoulder. The whole crew begged Keaton not to do it. The story editor wanted to quit. The cameraman filmed but had to look the other way. The director just walked off the set. The wall dropped...and the take was perfect. Not a drop of sweat marked Keaton's blank brow.

Before *Speed* (1994) hit the streets, before *Die Hard III* (1995) took to the tunnels, and before *The French Connection* (1971) ever connected, Buster Keaton tore up the tracks in his personal favorite, a Civil War–epic/chase comedy called *The General* (1927). Based, at least partially, on an 1862 Civil War train chase, Keaton's story features southern engineer Johnnie Gray ("The two loves of his life were his engine and Annabelle"), who is refused enlistment into the Confederate army. When Yankees steal his train, known as *The General*, with his gal on board, Johnnie takes off in one of the zaniest, most intricate, surreal, and death-defying pursuits imaginable. Not only is he the chaser on the way north, he's the chasee on the way back south. What a ride it was! As Keaton later said, "Railroads are a great prop. You can do some awfully wild things with railroads."

And wild they were in *The General*, with Keaton's character nearly being blown up by the malfunctioning of his own cannon car until a curve in the tracks makes magic happen. He sprints down the tracks on foot (a Keaton trademark), bicycle, and handcar at almost superhuman speed, practically surfing while filling the steam engine from a water tank. He straddles the cattle guard and plays tiddledywinks with the huge railroad ties that the bad guys have strewn on the tracks. He's so intent on stoking his engine for pursuit that he completely misses the columns of an advancing enemy army marching past. Who else could survive burning tunnels, falling bridges, crisscrossed tracks (using silky-smooth tracking shots before there ever was a Steadycam), a train that tends to wander away while he's looking for fuel in the nearby woods, and even a well-meaning southern belle (Marian Mack), who, during his desperate return flight while he dismantles the boxcar's own boards for fuel, blithely tosses away an imperfect board with a knothole in it? The master filmmaker even blows up a railroad bridge and a $42,000 train with it—praying that the first take works—in one of the greatest climaxes in film, let alone film comedy.

Genius that he was, Buster made what he later referred to as "the biggest mistake of my life" shortly after his acclaimed *Steamboat Bill Jr.*, when he allowed his brother-in-law Joseph M. Schneck to talk him into abandoning his own production company and signing on with MGM for $150,000 a year. While some of the MGM films, such as *The Cameraman* (1928), were worthy of his name, Keaton had no final authority and couldn't pick his own writers. The quality of the films deteriorated. Feeling trapped, Keaton began to drink steadily and became something of a womanizer, until his marriage broke under the strain. The talkies found his voice too flat, and his alcoholism ended his MGM contract.

Keaton never got back into the driver's seat. He survived, unappreciated and underpaid, by writing gags for Red Skelton, the Marx Brothers, and even Laurel and Hardy. He did bits in commercials and films (most notably, a brilliantly chaotic, clownish musical duo with Chaplin in *Limelight*). It wasn't until the late fifties and early sixties that the world rediscovered Keaton's classics, many of which had been feared lost. The Great Stone Face died on February 1, 1966, just as his comeback was at its peak. The genius' wry words on his final recognition were, "Sure, it's great but it's all thirty years too late."

The All-American Go-Getter in Glasses

In Fatty Arbuckle's Keystone short *Miss Fatty's Seaside Lovers*, a young bit player in the crowd does his best to shine amid the Sennett slapstick, though he does not quite fit in. A little earlier, the plucky, out-of-work stage actor named Harold Lloyd had "broken into" the Hollywood film biz by donning makeup and casually walking through Universal Studio's gates after a lunch break with the rest of the real extras, whom he had befriended. He didn't know it then, and he would slog through eighty to a hundred films before he really found himself, but that same inventiveness, planning, determination, and likableness would secure him as one of the most enduringly popular screen personas—not to mention wealthiest actors—in silent comedy.

Harold Lloyd, Hal to his pals, was the kind of boy to take home to meet the folks. No poverty, no abuse, just gosh-darn normality. Born in a frame house in Burchard, Nebraska, in 1893, Hal did a few magic tricks, a little boxing, and made a living schlepping for passing circuses and diving for money at the local pool.

An all-American, go-getting kid? Well, his mother did remember once hearing the voices of several kids playing on the porch, only to discover it was just Hal amusing himself. Her son also liked to line up hats and create characters for each chapeau. As an adolescent, he corralled kids into the basement stage that his father

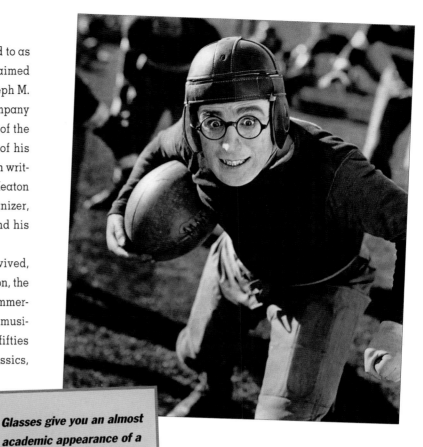

Now that's team spirit! Harold Lloyd is a sports maniac in **The Freshman** *(1925).*

> *Glasses give you an almost academic appearance of a studious man. But you don't necessarily have to be that. You can belie that appearance. You make it into a scrape, and they think you're very studious, and you do something entirely to dispel that idea. Well, you become a funny character because you don't do what they expect you to do.*
> —**Harold Lloyd, pragmatist and thrill-comedy genius**

(and future manager) had built, and for three cents admission for front-row seats and two cents for the back row, he treated them to his original play *Tom Morgan, the Cowboy of the West*.

Hal did a lot of stage work before coming to Hollywood. In 1911, when his unsuccessful entrepreneurial father was struck by a beer truck whose driver had been sampling his own wares, the $3,000 settlement financed a move for father and son to be determined by the flip of a coin—New York City or San Diego, California. The West won. While Hal (known as Speedy to his father, whom he called Foxy) toured in stock companies, playing mostly dramatic roles, Foxy's failed poolhall venture moved their home base to Los Angeles.

A dry spell on stage took Hal to the cameras. At Universal in 1915, he befriended a fellow $3-a-day extra named Hal Roach (they were eunuchs together in a three-reel version of *Samson*), and when Roach finagled a few thousand from the heir of a wealthy English family to start his own comedy studio, he brought the likable Hal along. When the studio's star comedian left after four failures, Roach turned to Lloyd and said, "Harold, you've got to be the low comedian. Think up something funny, and let's get busy."

They got busy, but it wasn't funny. Lloyd left for a stint with Mack Sennett's studio but returned to Roach (at $50 a week), and they tried again for a more salable commodity, *Lonesome Luke*.

Not bad for a guy with half a hand missing. The master of thrill comedy in perhaps the most famous scene from his most famous movie, Safety Last *(1923).*

With his size 12AA English shoes, a black-and-white-striped shirt, the coat from a woman's tailored suit, tight too-short pants and vest, cut-down hat, and two widely separated blobs of a mustache, Lonesome Luke was a popular but unremarkable trampish hero, a whimsical clone of a much more popular film clown.

In 1917, Lloyd saw a film about a fighting parson who wore glasses, which served to emphasize the parson's peaceable nature and the unreasonableness of the situation he found himself in. Lloyd had an idea, one that Roach also took credit for: "I would be an average, recognizable, American youth and let the situations take care of the comedy." A new character was born, one with no exaggerated makeup or features, just oversized horn-rims—The Boy.

The Boy was anything but average. The physical comedy Lloyd had learned at Keystone, paired with his athletic abilities— he was an avid boxer, bowler, golfer, tennis player, and handball player—made his Boy what one newspaper called "the human rubber ball." Through 1921, the savvy Lloyd made sure his Boy became a Saturday matinee staple, cranking out forty short films in 1919 alone (and making $1,000 a week plus a percentage of the profits).

When his first, lucky pair of glasses was no longer repairable, he shipped the glasses back to their eastern manufacturer for a new pair, only to receive twenty, gratis, with his check returned. His character had boosted horn-rim sales to new levels. As Chaplin was slowing his film output, Lloyd had become the comic that American audiences depended on and identified with. They also loved his increasing derring-do, whether vaulting over bicycles, midgets, and fences, then off a building and into a boat carrying a fat lady (*Why Pick on Me?*, 1918), hanging from a ledge by his fingernails (*High and*

Dizzy, 1920), or swinging from a noose tied to a high-rise girder (*Never Weaken*, 1921). The age of the thrill comedy had begun.

In 1919, it almost all ended. Prop man Frank Terry had grabbed a round, black bomb with a long, smoky, gag fuse on it from Roach's stock for a publicity photo session that Lloyd was doing. At the photographer's studio, Hal used it to light a cigarette, and the bomb detonated—for real. It had been part of a pair, inexpertly made up for an "uplifter's club" benefit. The second had been returned when the first shattered a heavy oak table to splinters. The prop's explosion tore a hole through the ceiling sixteen feet (4.9m) above his head, and every window in the studio had blown out with the impact. Lloyd had been temporarily blinded, his face seared, and the index finger and thumb of his right hand vaporized. A passing motorist hauled Lloyd and the injured photographer from the wreckage and took them to a hospital.

Luckily, Lloyd's personal character was not unlike his screen persona: the optimist would simply not give in. After a quick recovery, a prosthetic covered by a flesh-colored leather glove of the finest grain (one of the best-kept secrets in Hollywood) enabled Lloyd to go back into business, making the feature-length films for which he would be famous.

Why Worry? (1923) had him beautifully buddied up with—and pulling a tooth for—an eight-foot-six-inch (2.6m) giant named Johann Aasen. *Girl Shy* (1924) provided an unbelievable indoor-outdoor, out-of-control chase, with Lloyd manning a motorcycle, a streetcar, a wagon, and horses—occasionally with a chicken covering his face. *The Freshman* (1925) touched hearts and was the best college spoof ever shot. Yet the film Harold Lloyd is most remembered for is the story of ambition at a towering price, *Safety Last* (1923).

The idea for the film came to Lloyd one afternoon while watching "human fly" Bill Strothers climb an office building in downtown Los Angeles. Lloyd remembered, "The higher he climbed, the more nervous I grew, until when he came to a difficult ledge twelve stories up, I had to cut around the corner out of sight of him and peek back to see if he was over the ledge. 'If it makes me this jumpy, what would it do to a picture audience?' I asked myself."

Sure enough, Harold Lloyd would take every chance in *Safety Last*, the story of an ambitious department-store clerk who goes to insane, career-ruining lengths in order to convince his visiting hometown sweetheart that he is the general manager of his department store. On a less deluded level, this go-getter has also planned a building-climbing publicity stunt, which will win him $1,000. But when his best friend, the "human fly" (played by Strothers), is detained by the cops, the obsessed Lloyd has to make the thirteen-story climb himself.

Throughout Lloyd's ascent, the audience is always aware of the reality of the drop, as the frame continually includes the yawning chasm awaiting our hero's fall. His only safety net a tiny platform with a mattress on it as far as three stories beneath him (onto which the actor test-dropped a dummy, only to see it bounce and continue to plummet to the pavement), our hero encounters every conceivable, horrific, gag obstacle known to comedian on his nearly unwatchable way up.

From spilled water to a quintet of vicious pigeons, from tangling nets to tangling workmen, from hanging from a sprung clock face (one of silent movies' most famous stills and a stunt that caused Lloyd to throw out his shoulder) to gymnastics on tilting windows, from smashing into cornices to flailing around flagpoles, from dodging gunfire and lethal wind-gauges to freefalls, not to mention the smallest insult nature could create (which absolutely takes the cake), audiences laughed and gasped at this marvel of a film. It is a genuine climb that no thrill-seeking laugh seeker will want to miss. Does it have a happy ending? Of course, just as Lloyd's real life did. His dotage was spent out of the limelight in his thirty-two-room, $2.5 million Italian Renaissance villa known as Green Acres—66 acres (26.7ha) in all—in Benedict Canyon, one of Tinseltown's true showplaces. Harold Lloyd was indeed one clown who had the last laugh.

The Tradition Lives On

Silents gave audiences the first taste of film comedy, and though they don't play much today, the laughs they drew still reverberate. During the fifties and sixties, the brilliantly gawky Jacques Tati, a six-foot-four-inch (1.9m) French music-hall star and former pro rugby player, perfected a near-silent character with goofy charisma to rival the old masters.

Tati's storklike, pipe-smoking, head-in-the-air, calamity-creating Monsieur Hulot made a splash in a string of quirky, gag-packed (no one looks more nobly nonplussed sinking in a folding

TOP: Someone may well be following Monsieur Hulot (Jacques Tati) as he leaves a trail of comic chaos in Mon Oncle (1958). ABOVE: Dom DeLuise, Marty Feldman, and Mel Brooks (left to right) keep silent slapstick alive and well in Silent Movie (1976).

kayak or can be so funny filling up a watering can to put out a shed of exploding fireworks that he has set off), sound effects–filled films that leisurely find the humor of everyday people and their pursuits. *Monsieur Hulot's Holiday* (1952), *Mon Oncle* (1958), and *Playtime* (1968) were certified sensations the world over.

Director Mel Brooks—with a little help from actors such as Dom DeLuise, Marty Feldman, Bernadette Peters, Henny Youngman, and Harold Gould—perhaps paid highest homage to silent movies in his silent movie called *Silent Movie* (1976). This hysterical story of director Mel Funn and his attempt to revitalize silent comedy for Big Picture Studios ("If it's a big picture, we've made it!") is a veritable encyclopedia of sight gags that would have had Keaton rolling in the aisles—or taking notes.

The silent clown can keep on laughing, for budding filmmakers at film schools across the country cut their teeth on soundless cinema projects every year. And from every pratfall Chevy Chase and company ever brought to life on *Saturday Night Live* to the clownish characters of Italy's Roberto Benigni, it seems the joke isn't over yet.

Chapter Two

TEAMWORK

Two heads are better than one.

—Popular saying

They spell l-a-u-g-h-t-e-r pretty well, too. No one was better at revealing the child within all of us than Laurel and Hardy. Here, they play their own progeny in Brats (1930).

No comedian is an island. The likes of Chaplin, Keaton, and Lloyd may have shined on their own, but for countless other funny men and women, a partner made the laugh quotient increase exponentially. Ever since the Bard of Avon sent two collegiate clowns from the University of Wittenburg, Rosencrantz and Guildenstern, to cheer up and spy on a certain down-in-the-mouth prince of Denmark named Hamlet, only to have them bungle things so badly that they were executed under the very orders that were meant for their charge, comedy duos, trios, and troupes have been picking their way through life's minefields and making audiences explode with laughter in the process.

> *One is the loneliest number that you'll ever do.*
> *—"One" by Three Dog Night*

Long before cameras ever rolled, there were two basic types of clowns, and it was only natural that they would come together to cause as much trouble as possible. First, there was the white-faced scamp who made his first appearances in the circuses and equestrian shows of early nineteenth-century Europe. He was agile, energetic, fast-talking, aggressive, intelligent (relatively speaking), often outrageous, and always the perfect foil to the typically stodgy ringmaster. Robin Williams is a representative descendant.

By 1865, another clown had burst—well, more like tripped—upon the circus scene. The Auguste clown, with his oversize or undersize clothes, bulbous nose, and befuddled, sad-sack expression, didn't have a clue. His failed attempts to deal with the world around him and his tendency to wander into trouble made him lovable and hysterical. Steve Martin is the end of the line in that line. By the end of the century, pairings of white-faced clowns with Auguste clowns were turning up in circuses the world over, forerunners of the "straight man and fool" films to come.

The Boys

Okay, you've done something stupid, really stupid. Like pulling the rope that is not a doorbell but is pinned with a tag that reads "Caution: this ripcord will release 4,000 lbs. [1,814kg] of molasses, directly above you." Now, up to your waist in goo, do your eyes bug out? Do you holler and flail? Absolutely not. Staring straight ahead, trying to piece it together, you delicately pry off your gluey bowler, scratch your spiky hair, and then take a very long blink as you raise your eyebrows in a futile attempt at thought. As the stickiness of your situation dawns on you, you fiddle with your sticky hat, furrow your brow, and begin to blink back tears as your thin lips inaudibly mumble a high-pitched litany of distress.

"Now why is my leg feeling all wet?" wonders Oliver Hardy in Soup to Nuts (1928).

Or even better, your dim friend has done something really stupid, something having to do with molasses, and you were the lucky one standing next to him. Do you bellow and punch your pal in the nose? Do you plead for help from the man of the house, who has just opened the door? Don't be silly. You greet the gentleman, try to swell your ample girth and jowls with confidence, and twiddle your sodden tie. After casting a sidelong harumph at your partner, you give a long-suffering gaze out to the audience.

Two of filmdom's favorite clowns, perhaps the most beloved duo in screen history, put a uniquely genteel mark on team comedy that can never be erased. They remain so popular that, more than half a century after their heyday, dozens of chapters of the Sons of the Desert society exist, solely to worship their work; their unmistakable images have been borrowed by impersonators in dozens of commercials and ads, not to mention by other comedy greats such as Dick Van Dyke; and worldly giants like Franklin Delano Roosevelt, Winston Churchill, and Benito Mussolini had all been known to kick back in times of stress with private screenings of their films. Their stately pace and almost childlike good fellowship have given generations of comedians permission to put down their brickbats to explore the child within.

Laurel and Hardy didn't start off together—far from it. In fact, just before their pairing, Stan Laurel had about had it with the

NOTHING TO LAUGH ABOUT

Comedy—the hilarious ones take it very seriously. Let's see what some of them have to say about the cruel mistress of mirth that they slave for.

"All comedians have the same kinship as women in childbirth."
—Georgie Jessel

"If what you're doing is funny, you don't have to be funny doing it."
—Charlie Chaplin

"To become real successful, they must like you very much....They must have a feeling like, 'Gee I wish he was a friend of mine. I wish he were a relative.' "
—Jack Benny

"I'm a classic example of all humorists—only funny when I'm working."
—Peter Sellers

"Comedy you are born with or not born with. If you have it then you can create it automatically. All you need is practice. It's like playing tennis: you have to keep your arm and your eye to remain efficient."
—Woody Allen

"Making yourself look stupid seems much more human. Making other people look stupid just looks cheap."
—Steve Martin

"Comedy is serious—deadly serious. Never, never try to be funny! The actors must be serious. Only the situation must be absurd."
—Mel Brooks

"The thing about comedy is that there's no sanctity in it. It goes straight to the nerve that's not supposed to be tickled, straight to the thing that's not supposed to be talked about."
—Jim Carrey

"When you're a leading man, the dames chase you. When you're a comic, the kids chase you."
—Harold Frazer (a.k.a. Snub Pollard), a Hal Roach comedian famed for his hysterical, gadget-oriented comedy

"I have a file of four million jokes. I don't know if you know that. I have them cross-indexed. Whatever subject you want, I have a joke on it. They're in my vault, in my files. They're willed to the Library of Congress."
—Milton Berle

"Most great comedians were great athletes. Physical humor demands rhythm and timing. I love making people think I've just killed myself."
—Chevy Chase

"People think that all I have to do is stand up here and tell a few jokes. Well, that's not as easy as it looks. Every year it gets to be more of an effort to stand up."
—George Burns

"The refrigerator light goes on and I do twenty minutes."
—Jerry Lewis

"A lot of us have hatred and pain in us—all the things that make good actors."
—Eddie Murphy

"Comedy, like sodomy, is an unnatural act."
—Marty Feldman

"I think the kind of comedy I rebelled against was the joke-telling, where the material was everything."
—Buster Keaton

"All the comedian has to show for his years is the echo of forgotten laughter."
—Fred Allen

"I can't do comedy."
—Marlon Brando

"If at first you don't succeed, try again. Then quit—no use in being a damn fool about it."
—W.C. Fields

movie business. When Charlie Chaplin had crossed over to the United States with Fred Karno's Music Hall revue in 1912, Stan had been his understudy and stayed stateside to tour his own solo vaudeville act. When one of the theater owners took a shot at the budding film business and starred Stan in a short called *Nuts in*

May (1917), he was snapped up by Universal Studios and quickly given starring roles. But unlike Chaplin, Laurel could not quickly create a screen persona that made him a household item.

Like so many other vaudevillians, he was fast, sharp, funny, lithe, irreverent, and girl-chasing, and he even laughed at his own gags—as did most comedians. After only a handful of films at Universal, Stan was back in vaudeville, and for the next decade he worked on and off in movies. By 1926, the creative but frustrated Laurel was ready to take a stab at writing and directing for Hal Roach Studios.

Meanwhile, Oliver Norvell Hardy from Atlanta, Georgia, had been going through frustration of his own. Babe, as he was known to his friends (thanks to an Italian barber who liked to powder his ample chins like the bottom of a baby), had been a big kid (weighing in at 250 pounds [113kg] at fourteen years of age) with a nice voice who got roped into his film debut one day in 1913 while he was a spectator at the Lubin Studios in Florida. Soon Hardy was playing second-string villains. He even held a young Stan Laurel at gunpoint in the cowboy picture *A Lucky Dog* (1917). Only after the horse he was riding collapsed under his weight into a sand dune during filming in 1924 at Roach Studios was Hardy assigned exclusively to play comedy.

> *One for all and all for one.*
> **—The Three Musketeers**

That other early comedy producing/directing titan, ex–truck driver Hal Roach, whose studio's relaxed and creative atmosphere depended less on slapstick and more on imagination and character, needed a comedy sensation to fill the gap left by Harold Lloyd, who had gone on to make his own films. From a hodgepodge called the Hal Roach All Stars, Laurel and Hardy stood out as a possible pair. Roach gave them the secret recipe for success that he gave all his comics: "Emulate the actions of children." Not bad advice, considering that Roach's group of child actors, the Little Rascals, were delighting audiences everywhere.

It wasn't until their seventh film together that Laurel found the child within and a slower gear of subserviency, allowing Hardy to take charge in

his famously lame yet fastidious way. In *Putting the Pants on Philip* (1927), Hardy plays Piedmont Mumblethunder, the best-dressed man in Upper Sandusky and uncle to Laurel's boobish, kilt-wearing young Scotsman, whom he practically has to hog-tie to get measured for a proper suit. From then on, the duo—under the direction of thirty-one-year-old Roach fledgling Leo McCarey—was, in Hardy's own words, "two minds without a single thought." Stan removed the heels from a pair of heavy shoes to get that famous flatfooted waddle for his singularly slowed character. Ollie perfected his nit-picking and famously lame brand of authority. They were dismal domestics in *Soup to Nuts* (1928) and model prisoners in *Pardon Us* (1931). They doubled as their own children in *Brats* (1930), their own sisters (each married to the other) in *Twice Two* (1933), and their own brothers (sailors, both) in *Our Relations* (1936).

One of their most famous—and destructive—shorts was *Two Tars* (1928), in which "The Boys" (as they came to be known around the studio) are sailors on shore leave who take two girls for a ride in a rented car, only to create a monster pile-up on the California highway (even back then). In another film, *Big Business* (1929), The Boys are Christmas-tree salesmen in July who are taking advance orders. Their spirited pitch and blunders with a homeowner, played by James Finlayson, quickly degenerate to total warfare as The Boys end up making as big a mess

ABOVE: Stan and Stanella? Brother and sister in Twice Two (1933). LEFT: "The Boys" and the man who made them rich men, producer Hal Roach.

of Finlayson's house as he does their car and sample trees.

Ironically, this time the destruction had a note of reality. Roach's studio was under pressure to finish *Big Business* by Christmas week 1928 so that the studio could close down to install its new sound equipment. Roach's brainstorm was to use an employee's bungalow as the location and give him and his family a paid vacation and a handsome fee while he wrecked their house. Unfortunately, the first day of shooting took the Roach crew to a house just up the street, whose occupants also happened to be on vacation. Finding the door locked, the crew decided to bust it down and, in the shooting days ahead, demolished much of the exterior. By the time the owners came back, Roach had cut the heads off all the trees in their yard, as well. Oops! Up went the budget.

The Boys' transition to sound was a smooth one. Their Oscar for Best Live-Action Comedy Short for *The Music Box* in 1932 (a muddle-brained moving man's nightmare) spurred them on to celebrated features like *Sons of the Desert* (1933), in which they played henpecked husbands followed by their wives to a lodge convention in Chicago. In perhaps their last great feature, *Blockheads* (1938), Stan is a doggedly dim World War I sentry who has been guarding the same military post since 1917 (with a mountain of bean tins beside it). Ollie is married to a wife who keeps him on an allowance of seventy-five cents a day. On his wedding anniversary, he reads about Stan's admittance to a veteran's hospital, and impulsively goes to rescue him. During their tearful reunion Stan is lounging in a wheelchair with leg tucked up under him and Ollie, assuming he's an amputee, insists on lugging a bewildered Stan to his wife's car—which they proceed to wreck in sensational fashion, a cement truck adding the finishing touch.

Back at Ollie's thirteenth-floor apartment—and after one of the most mishap-strewn and laborious climbs imaginable—The Boys set about whipping up a little something to eat (Stan suggests beans)...and let's just say apartment insurance would have been handy. A sequence was eventually dropped in which the two bring back a drunk whom they can only make intelligible by shaking him when he talks. He misuses the bathroom plumbing so severely that when the boys notice water leaking out the bathroom keyhole and they open the door, a wall of water carries them right

back down the thirteen flights out into the street. Luckily, the remaining bits embroiling Hardy's beautiful and good-natured neighbor, Mrs. Gilbert (Patricia Ellis), in further chaos with his domineering wife and Mrs. Gilbert's insanely jealous, big game–hunting husband, are inspired upheaval.

Upheaval also described the conditions under which this last great movie was made. While Babe, the avid sportsman, was raising racehorses and betting as much as $7,000 on the golf matches he played with buddies such as Bing Crosby, Johnny Weismuller, and W.C. Fields, Laurel had energetically involved himself in every aspect of writing, production, and direction. Although Stan had invented priceless gags on the set (like smoking his hand as a pipe or finding a glass of water in one pocket and ice cubes in another), he was enmeshed in a crumbling marriage to a fractious Russian blues singer named Illiana, who claimed during their divorce proceedings that her husband had dug an open grave and invited her to step in.

Roach claimed that the depressed Laurel was drunk on the set, and Laurel left town in a huff before filming was finished. As a result, the ending Laurel had planned—in which his and Hardy's heads are stuffed and mounted on Mr. Gilbert's trophy wall, with Ollie saying, "Well, here's another fine mess you've gotten us into"—was scrapped. Director John G. Blystone died of a heart attack during the final cut, and Roach himself crafted a new ending

These Sons of the Desert (1933) are in a bit of hot water.

where The Boys (their doubles, actually) flee down the alley from the rifle-blasting hunter, who screams, "I'll teach you to fool around with my wife!" At the threat, dozens of other adulterers climb out of neighboring fire escapes and hightail it, too. Now that's an exit.

The Great Miscommunicators, or "I'm a B-a-a-a-d Boy!"

Another offshoot from minstrel shows was burlesque (from *burla*, the Italian term for "jest"). Burleycue, as it was affectionately nicknamed, got its start as the third part of every minstrel show, a series of musical and nonmusical parodies of events and people of the day. Early American burlesque offered entire shows of parody and satire. In time, with the competition from wholesome vaudeville, and sell-out hits like Ziegfeld's *Follies*, burlesque was compelled to up the ante with an emphasis on "leg shows"—dance numbers revealing various amounts of female anatomy, and more sexually explicit fare from the comics who, like their vaudeville counterparts, stood before the curtain and cracked jokes while the girls got dressed (or undressed) for their next number. Famous

funnymen such as Phil Silvers and Red Buttons got their start in this savory yet unsavory environment. But the most famous duo it ever produced was the fast-talking team of Abbott and Costello.

They met at the Minsky Theater on 2nd Avenue in New York City one night in 1936 when the twenty-nine-year-old comic, a former prize-fighter and, yes, former double for Dolores Del Rio, named Lou Costello found himself minus a straight man. The son of circus performers, Bud Abbott, a former shanghaied teenage sailor, and a then–vaudeville house cashier, filled the gap, and lightning struck. Abbott's peerless patter, staccato delivery, sharp looks, and all-business seriousness were the perfect complement to the chubby, cherubic, chumpy, daff-and-a-half Costello.

Mining more than two hundred established vaudeville routines revolving around not physical but verbal misunderstandings, the duo did the vaudeville and burlesque circuits, wowing audiences with perfectly timed renditions of classics like the now famous "Who's on First?" Bud got 60 percent of the take to Lou's 40 percent—a straight man was a much more precious commodity than a comic. Thanks to a 1938 break from airwave personality Kate Smith, the two quickly had their own popular radio show. From there, they moved on to Broadway to become the toast of the town in revues like *The Streets of Paris* with Carmen Miranda.

In 1940, largely thanks to Lou's desire to return to Hollywood as something more than a starlet's double, Abbott and Costello were featured in their first film, *One Night in the Tropics*. The following year, as the United States edged into World War II, Bud and Lou made five smash films for Universal Studios, including the musical comedy hit *Buck Privates* (in which the pair, on the run after a tie-selling scam, hide out in what is not a movie line but an enlistment line), followed by *In the Navy* and *Keep 'Em Flying*. Wartime audiences had found the perfect diversion, and rumor has it that the Japanese High Command showed the films to their troops as a morale booster, telling them Bud and Lou were typical American GIs.

In five short years, the twosome had skyrocketed from obscurity to find themselves among Hollywood's top-ten box-office draws. By the time they made *Rio Rita* (1942), they were all-time box-office champs. And they made good on their celebrity, not by filming a defense drama only on war bonds, but by selling $80 million of them during one cross-country tour. Their treasure trove of routines was so ingrained in each of them that they could improvise like mad over a secure structure, letting their crisp delivery make every old bit seem fresh. Though Lou was suffering from rheumatic fever on his thirty-seventh birthday, the duo was back up and running after a year's bedrest and was rolling them in the aisles through the mid-1940s with hits like *Hit the Ice* (1943), *Lost in a Harem* (1944), and *The Naughty Nineties* (1945).

Lou (left) and Bud joined up with the Andrews Sisters in the all-singing, all-dancing, all-laughing Buck Privates *(1941).*

It Was a Dark and Pastrami Night!

When Abbott and Costello's star finally started to fade, Universal Studios made one of the boldest and weirdest yet most fortunate moves in movie history: they teamed the team with a lycanthrope, a vampire, and a seven-foot (2.1m) monster—plus a couple of beautiful girls. After all, producer Robert Arthur reasoned, the studio already owned the rights to the once-popular characters of *The Wolf Man* (1941), *Dracula* (1930), and *Frankenstein* (1931). Suppose Dracula had taken possession of the Frankenstein monster. Suppose the problem with its previous brain was that it had been too strong and aggressive. Suppose he needed a pliable, feeble, childlike brain to control the monster. Where could he find one? Oh, Lou!

The original and even weirder treatment was more along these lines: Abbott and Costello are two stewards aboard an ocean liner who meet up with a mysterious Doctor Fell. The doc, it seems, has the bodies of Frank, Wolfie, and Drac back at his New York museum and has stolen the secret of how to reanimate them from the Baroness Von Frankenstein. The secret is microfilmed in a matchbook, which he pawns off on the duo to get it off the ship for him. They lose the matchbook, and the film follows it from person to person as they try to get it back, and eventually everybody ends up at the museum. It turns out that vinegar will reawaken Frank, baked beans will revive Wolfie, and a stake pulled out of Dracula's skeleton will do the trick for him. So, of course, Bud and Lou sit down in the museum kitchen to a meal of baked beans with vinegar and pull this piece of wood out of a skeleton to prop up their table. Their messy eating dribbles on the respective monsters, and voilà! Only the arrival of the baroness, with an atomizer that shrinks each creature to four inches (10.2cm) tall, saves the day. As a reward, she allows Bud and Lou to exhibit the trio in a Broadway show, with the stern warning not to let olives come in contact with any of them. Of course, Lou is snarfing a deli sandwich backstage when....

Nix! Two treatments later, shipping clerk Wilbur Gray (Lou) is inexplicably and amorously pursued by both sexy European doctor Sandra Mornay (Lenore Albert) and gorgeous, wholesome Joan Raymond (Jane Randolph). Turns out that Sandra works for Dracula, who has been shipped in a huge crate (along with Frank) to a New York museum. She now wants Wilbur's brain in order to reanimate the monster. Joan is an insurance investigator trying to get to the bottom of it by woo-

ABOVE: Bela Lugosi didn't exactly have to strain to penetrate the tiny mind of Lou Costello in the hilarious **Abbott and Costello Meet Frankenstein** *(1948).* BELOW: Lon Chaney, Jr., is only trying to give Lou a friendly warning in **Abbott and Costello Meet Frankenstein.**

ing Wilbur. Wilbur is in seventh heaven, but fellow clerk Chick Young (Bud Abbott) is mystified and irritated by his partner's new-found magnetism. Meanwhile, a tortured Lawrence Talbot (a.k.a. Wolfie) is trying to warn the dim duo of the peril they face.

Lou was not exactly crazy about the script. He stormed into the Universal production office yelling, "My daughter could write a better script than this! You're not serious about it, are you?" They were. They had even procured the services of Lon Chaney, Jr., Bela Lugosi, and Glen Strange to portray the three creatures. The horror was to be played very, very seriously. As Bela boasted, "There is no burlesque for me. All I have to

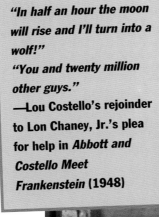

"In half an hour the moon will rise and I'll turn into a wolf!"
"You and twenty million other guys."
—Lou Costello's rejoinder to Lon Chaney, Jr.'s plea for help in *Abbott and Costello Meet Frankenstein* (1948)

do is frighten the boys, a perfectly appropriate activity! My trademark will be unblemished."

Makeup wizard Bud Westmore altered the classic Jack Pierce's original designs (with spongelike rubber mask pieces) to reduce Chaney's makeup application from four hours to one and Strange's from six hours to one. Ironically, Chaney graciously did double-duty at one point (having played Frank himself in *The Ghost of Frankenstein*, 1942) when Strange suffered a fractured ankle after throwing Sandra through a breakaway window only to have her bounce back and send him flying.

There were real gags, too. The five-week shoot expanded to seven with all the shenanigans. For starters, Abbott and Costello had their own personal stooge, Bobby Barber, on the set, whom they paid $25 a day to keep them entertained. Practical jokes were rampant. Bobby dropped an egg on director Charlie Barton's head from the soundstage rafters. Lou built a fire under Bobby's chair. Barber would arrive in an outlandish golfing costume and shave his socks with an electric razor during filming. With hundreds of dollars in purchased custard pies (for throwing, not eating), exploding cigars, and seltzer bottles (for spraying, not drinking), who wouldn't have a good time? Even Lenore got into the act when she decked herself out in a mink wrap, put a leash on Frankenstein, and walked him around the Universal lot—much to the shock of visiting tourists.

Bud's and Lou's children were also regular visitors to the playpen and loved watching the monsters casually eating, drinking, and smoking off-camera. Lou, true to form, stole a clock from the mantel in Dracula's castle and had to be bribed to return it. There were boo-boos, the most blatant being Dracula reflected in Sandra's mirror. In another scene, where Bud and Lou are on one side of a door when the monster punches through it, Lou, who never paid much attention to marks, was off his and got Strange's fist right in the nose. And during a chase around a secret door, Lou yells, "Abbott!" when he should have been yelling "Chick!"

Despite all the horsing around, this movie is a perfect blend of scary and funny. Lou's fear, which Abbott, of course, completely dismisses, is classic Costello. And Lou as *homme fatal* is a concept almost too funny to think about. *Abbott and Costello Meet Frankenstein* turned out to be the second-cheapest production in 1948 and quickly made $800,000 at the box office. Lou still hated it, even though his mother told him it was the best thing that he had ever done. *The Dayton* (Ohio) *Journal* echoed those sentiments in a slightly different way: "One thing we can say...is that all the monsters aren't on the screen. Pint-sized ones surrounded us at yesterday's matinee, and their blood-curdling shrieks, their guffaws, their shouted instructions and their frenzied, weird bodily contortions as the hapless heroes stumbled from horror to horror, will haunt us long after the final fill fades from our memories."

During a preview, when producer Robert Arthur saw how much the audience loved it, he turned to the duo after the ending—in which they are rescued by the Invisible Man—and said, "That's your next picture."

Minnie's Madmen

Minnie Schoenberg Marx had high hopes for her boys. Her own father, Lafe, a ventriloquist and magician in the old country (Germany), had been reduced to repairing umbrellas in the States. Her mother, Fanny, had been a yodeling harpist. She agented her brother Al, who had changed his last name to Shean, joined a fellow named Mr. Gallagher, and became a singing, joke-telling staple of the vaudeville stage. She had bigger plans for her sons, Leonard (b. 1887), Adolph (b. 1888), Julius (b. 1890), Milton (b. 1897), and Herbert (b. 1901). As Adolph later reminisced, "She was a lovely woman, but her soft, doelike looks were deceiving. She had the stamina of a brewery horse, the drive of a salmon fighting his way up a waterfall, the cunning of a fox, and a devotion to her brood as fierce as any she-lion's."

Minnie played the guitar, and her husband, Sam "Frenchie" Marx (whom she met at a dancing school), played the mandolin. Before the turn of the century, she was sending Leonard, thereafter known as Chico (for his interest in chicks), to piano lessons at a whopping twenty-five cents a pop. Chico was supposed to teach Adolph, later known as Harpo (for his harp playing), everything he had learned in his lessons, but he was too busy hustling money and betting it. (As the rechristened Groucho said later, "There are three things that my brother Chico is always on—a phone, a horse, or a broad.")

Harpo turned his musical attention to his grandmother's old harp, leaving the second grade after the school bully dropped him once too often from his classroom's second-story window. He worked throughout his childhood as a hot-dog seller, a bellboy, a junk seller, a celebrity dog–walker, and even a pin setter at the local bowling alley.

Julius, known as Groucho for his often grumpy demeanor, was the most studious, serious, and responsible of the brood, with intentions of going to medical school—intentions he dropped when he left school at the age of thirteen. Among other jobs, he worked

One of the greatest vocalists of our time, Harpo Marx (standing) delivers one of his famous arias in the Marx Brothers'
Animal Crackers (1930).

as a delivery boy for a company that sold wigs—wigs that Harpo used to borrow. At home, he contributed his guitar-playing and singing talents to the music fests that the Marxes enjoyed. As the years went by, Groucho became a boy singer with vaudeville's Le May Trio, touring for $4 a week plus room and board.

Harpo, who had taught himself piano without Chico's help, was playing at a Long Island brothel, where he got fired for getting too friendly with the employees. Chico entered vaudeville as a blindfolded accompanist for his cousin, Lou Shean, and one summer he actually replaced a pianist named George Gershwin at a New York beer garden.

Minnie brought her musical geniuses together and put them on the road when she formed the Four Nightingales, a harmony act minus Chico, which included Milton, known as Gummo (for his gumsoled shoes), and an Irish lass named Jane O'Reilly. Though Harpo supposedly wet his pants his first time onstage, the Four Nightingales set off cross-country. Destiny struck in the unlikely wilds of east Texas.

The audience in Nacogdoches, Texas, was less than attentive, and when news of a runaway mule all but vacated the theater, the

Marx Brothers became exasperated enough to start sending up their own songs and hurling rapid-fire insults to the yokels in the audience. Lines such as "Nacogdoches is full of roaches" made the locals laugh and cheer. The boys had hit on something. A little later, in Dennison, Texas, performing for a teachers' convention, they spontaneously decided to do a professorial skit with a German-accented Groucho in a frock coat, glasses, and a painted mustache (he couldn't find a crepe one); a wig-topped Harpo played a moronic bumpkin named Patsy Branigan. When they got back from touring, Chico joined the pack as Leo the Wop (picking up an Italian accent, as Groucho dropped his German one in light of pre–WWI resentment, and picked up a cigar) with Uncle Al Shean writing music and skits for the boys. In one of these, Harpo only had three lines; the review of the act touted Harpo as a brilliant mime but complained that the magic was lost each time he opened his mouth. He never sneezed onstage or onscreen again—except in *At the Circus* (1939).

Viva Anarchy! Hail Freedonia! Look out Below!

Take the Marx Brothers. Take out the harp and piano solos. Nix the romantic interest. Add the plotting guidance and creative control of veteran director Leo McCarey. Add dowager queen and honorary fifth Marx Brother Margaret Dumont. Heat with nonstop gags and ridicule everything military and pompously diplomatic. Distill it to its essence...and you have what most fans believe to be the

> It was I who introduced my wife to the Marx Brothers' films and she is now as keen a fan as I am.
> —T.S. Eliot

purest expression of Marxian madness ever produced, or, as Groucho explained, the recipe that resulted in the film's title: "Take two turkeys, one goose, four cabbages, but no duck, and mix them together. After one taste, you'll duck soup the rest of your life."

While *Monkey Business* (1931) took potshots at film noir, and *Horse Feathers* (1932) lambasted the groves of academe, *Duck Soup* (1933) set itself in the European nation of Freedonia, which was enmeshed in political intrigue and eventual war with its neighbor, Sylvania. Rufus T. Firefly (Groucho) was its wayward leader, and Pinky (Harpo) and Chicolini (Chico) were two spies for the other side.

With Adolf Hitler's then-recent appointment as chancellor of Germany (Harpo would change his own name to Arthur), the Nazi terror beginning in earnest, Mussolini's fascists in power in Italy, and America three years into its Great Depression, the world was not the cocksure place it had been during the 1920s. Shaken audiences were ripe for the laughs that the Marx Brothers were about to dish out at the expense of foreign tyrants.

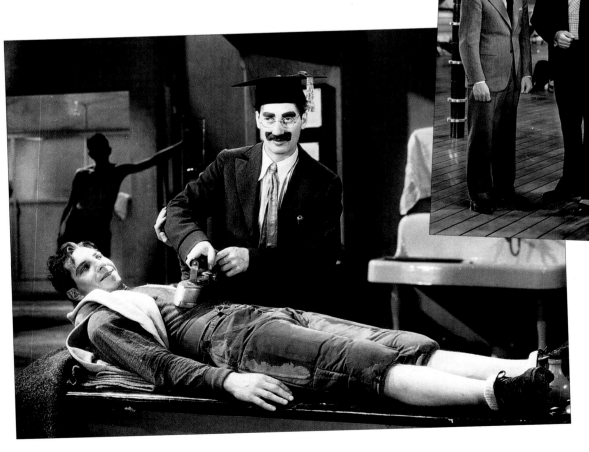

LEFT: As president of Huxley College, Groucho is set on getting a winning football team; he's also willing to do a little ironing for his brother Zeppo in Horse Feathers *(1932). ABOVE: Groucho (right) shows Thelma Todd that she isn't the only tough cookie on the ship in* Monkey Business *(1931).*

Are these a couple of master spies or what? Chicolini (Chico) likes Pinky's (Harpo) hat in Duck Soup (1933).

The brothers were riding high and wild coming into *Duck Soup*, and they were a little out of control, even for the Marx Brothers. Groucho and Chico were fresh from a New York–based radio show that folded after twenty-six weeks—following Groucho's commentary of their two illustrious sponsors, Corn Flakes and Standard Oil: "If you're hungry some morning, you might try this combination." On the Paramount set, Chico, Harpo, Groucho, and Zeppo (Herbert, so named because of his proclivity for doing chin-ups like a vaudeville monkey act called Zippo) horsed around, playing darts while the writers wrote. When they got bored, the quartet decided it was time to work and commanded the writers to come in for a meeting at 9:30 the next morning. "But we always come in at 9:30," said the writers. "Well, then come in at 8:30," the brothers responded.

The next morning, Bert Kalmar and Harry Ruby (who had also collaborated on *Animal Crackers*, 1930, *Horse Feathers*, 1932, and such signature songs as "Hooray for Captain Spaulding") were there at 8:30, but the brothers didn't waltz in until 11:45. Before the writers could gripe, the Marx mob charged, "Where were you?" The writers said, "Where were we? We were right here!" The Marxes replied, "How do you like that, they were right here. We go out of our way to have a meeting and they just sit here!" "Well, wait a minute," protested Ruby. "Look, Harry," interjected Groucho, "we're making a picture and spending a lot of money, and when we say 9:30, we mean business." Kalmar stammered, "Well, wait a minute, Groucho, where were you guys?" "Why, RKO!" harumphed Groucho. "RKO?" queried Kalmar incredulously. "We're not making this picture for RKO!" "Don't change the subject!" snapped Groucho.

Boys will be boys. Even thirty-four-year-old McCarey was initially at wit's end. The Marx Brothers had a clause in their contract that they never had to film after 6 P.M.; if McCarey tried to make the late-arriving zanies work into the evening, they'd yell, "Read my contract!" Finally, McCarey fought fire with fire: starting a juicy scene in mid-afternoon, he got the boys primed and in their stride just before he walked off the set and went home, letting his assistant call to reassure the dumbfounded quartet that he'd be back and fresh the next morning.

> *Cedric Hardwicke is my fifth favorite actor, the first four being the Marx Brothers.*
> —George Bernard Shaw

> *If you were asked to name the best comedies ever made and you named* The Gold Rush *and* The General, *and a half a dozen others, Duck Soup is the only one that really doesn't have a dull spot.*
> —Woody Allen

Hired guns such as Nat Perrins and Grover Jones were brought in to make *Duck Soup* the most gag-crammed movie the Marx Brothers had ever made. Groucho claimed that he always tried each gag out on Zeppo; if he laughed, into the trash it went. But what gags they were. The comic mayhem includes the famous mirror bit with Groucho and Harpo both dressed as Groucho. McCarey himself instigated the classic silent battle between lemonade vendor (Edgar Kennedy) and roasted-peanut vendor (Harpo). There's Harpo's most devastating prop ever, an uncontrollable pair of scissors. The war itself is one of the last places you'd expect to see the Marx Brothers, and their spiritual number, "They got guns; We got guns; All God's children got guns," is beyond ludicrous.

Other, stranger gems were cut by the judicious McCarey. A tango race for Freedonia's war plans bit the dust. Firefly no longer pulled a rabbit out of a hat at every entrance and exit. The tattoo on Harpo's chest that originally depicted an outhouse became a doghouse with a barking dog. A Groucho song vanished that would have yielded, "Of course, you're all aware that a king must have an heir. Someone to pass the family name along. Will someone tell me where I'll ever get an heir if a king can do no wrong."

HEY, LOOK, IT'S GOMER PYLE!

Johnny Weismuller gave us Tarzan. Anthony Perkins gave us Norman Bates. Sean Connery gave us Bond, James Bond. Clint Eastwood gave us the Man with No Name. Throughout the history of comedy, some comedians have also been identified as much, if not more, with their movie or television monikers than with their real ones. See if you can connect the handles (and a hint or two) with the humans behind them.

EGO

1) Julia Sweeney
2) Paul Rubens
3) Cliff Arquette
4) Roland Young
5) Michael Keaton
6) Mike Myers
7) Henry Winkler
8) Samuel Horowitz
9) Lincoln Theodore Monroe Andrew Perry
10) George Emmett McFarland
11) Mickey Rooney
12) Jackie Gleason
13) Jim Henson
14) Rick Moranis
15) Harris Glenn Milstead
16) Peter Sellers
17) Carroll O'Connor
18) Jim Varney
19) Jim Backus
20) Mel Blanc
21) Lily Tomlin

ALTER EGO

A) Ernestine (snorting telephone operator)
B) Ernest (goat-faced gum head)
C) Andy Hardy (all-American)
D) Ralph Cramden (bellicose bus driver)
E) Divine (John Waters' Big Mama)
F) Kermit the Frog (green crooner)
G) Porky Pig (barnyard stutterer)
H) Inspector Clouseau (defective detective)
I) Archie Bunker (beloved bigot)
J) Thurston Howell III (cultured castaway)
K) Beetlejuice (ghost with the most)
L) The Fonz (50s favorite)
M) Charlie Weaver (Hollywood "Square")
N) Bob McKenzie (Canadian beer connoisseur)
O) Shemp (professional Stooge)
P) Stepin Fetchit (servile stereotype)
Q) Pat (annoyingly androgynous)
R) Wayne Campbell (basement teen star)
S) Pee-Wee Herman (kooky kid clown)
T) Topper (sport for the spirits)
U) Spanky (chubby child star)

Answers: 1=Q, 2=S, 3=M, 4=K, 5=T, 6=R, 7=L, 8=O, 9=P, 10=U, 11=C, 12=D, 13=F, 14=N, 15=E, 16=H, 17=I, 18=B, 19=J, 20=G, 21=A

Firefly's caustic lines to and about wealthy widow Mrs. Teasedale (Dumont) alone are worth the price of admission—lines such as "Remember, we're fighting for this woman's honor, which is probably more than she ever did." Suffice it to say that there's enough there to keep you occupied while you roll on the floor in hysterics.

Regarding that condition, during a screening of the rushes, a nervous Kalmar turned to Chico and asked, "Well, do you think they'll like it?" "Like it? Look, they'll piss," Chico replied. "No doubt about that," an eavesdropping Groucho added, "but will they laugh?"

They laughed, but not enough. Though purists today agree that *Duck Soup* represents Marxian madness at its height, critical acclaim in 1933 was mixed enough for Paramount to drop the Marx Brothers' contract, sending them to the more managerial arms of Irving Thalberg at MGM—and in came the romance and the harp solos. On the plus side, dictator Mussolini banned the film in Italy. And he wasn't the only public official upset: shortly after it opened, the mayor of a certain Fredonia, New York, wrote Groucho to complain: "The name of Fredonia has been without blot since 1817. I feel it is my duty as mayor to question your intentions in using the name of our city in your picture." Groucho wrote back, as only Groucho would dare: "Your excellency. Our advice is to change the name of your town. It is hurting our picture. Anyhow, what makes you think you're mayor of Fredonia? Do you wear a black mustache; play a harp; speak with an Italian accent or chase girls, like Harpo? We are certain you do not. Therefore, we must be mayor of Freedonia, not you." The old gray mayor ain't what he used to be.

The Dazzlers

When he died in early 1995, many people remembered Peter Cook as one of the funniest human beings who had ever lived: the Englishman whose deadly dry wit and consummate character writing inspired a generation of Britain's best comic minds. At least that's what John Cleese, also one of the funniest men who has ever lived, acknowledged.

The short one agreed in the assessment. Dudley Moore brought the tall one's lines and characters to life. While the short one and the tall one were together from 1960 to 1977, their bizarre sketch material and razor-sharp characters were a force to be reckoned with. Though most noted for stage and television work, their true star turn together in Stanley Donen's *Bedazzled* (1967) makes it among the funniest films ever made—and rented all too rarely.

Peter Cook (the son of a member of the Foreign Office) and Dudley Moore (a working-class boy who wanted to be an organist) first met during college. Dudley was acting in plays and studying music at Oxford. Meanwhile, at Cambridge University, Pete was already writing for the Footlights Club with such collegiate contributors as England's future shining playwright Harold Pinter. Writing was nothing new to Cook, who had been a contributor of bogus news articles to the humor magazine *Punch* since he was ten.

As did many good Anglo collegiate comedians and thespians, Pete 'n' Dud attended Scotland's Edinburgh Festival in the summer of 1960, where an assistant director put them together with two other actor-writer types, Alan Bennett (future author of such plays as *The Madness of King George III*), and ex-Cambridgian and practicing neurologist Jonathan Miller (future surgeon, BBC science-show host, and director of Laurence Olivier's *The Merchant of Venice*), to slap together a late-night cabaret. What the foursome created for their two weeks in Scotland was an evening's entertainment that swept not only the festival, but England and America, eventually winning the 1962 Tony for Best Play. *Beyond the Fringe*—with its quirky combination of biting social satire, dry wit, and ludicrous situations and characters—became one of the hottest tickets in the western hemisphere.

They hit English television screens with the 1964, 1966, and 1970 sketch series, *Not Only...But Also* (not only but also available on videotape), which included sundry now-infamous skits: a deadpan English lord

> "I used to be cynical when I was young: but by God it's worse now."
> —Peter Cook

(Cook) telling his nervous, nebbishy, nineteen-year-old son (Moore) the most macabre and inaccurate facts of life imaginable (something to do with warm leather chairs and cats); an antiseptic Oxfordian analysis of soul music lyrics (mama's got a new bag = an infant's mother buys a gaily colored new shopping bag on the quaint streets of Harlem); a hilarious takeoff of a marionette-populated sci-fi show for the kiddies (SUPERTHUNDERSTINGCAR); Ludwig van Beethoven as a pop star (his covers of Tom Jones' hits are something to hear); a completely cocked Greta Garbo bioflick (with Cook in drag); and repeated side-splitting scenes of two befuddled drinking buddies (Pete 'n' Dud) and their skewed musings on everything from modern art to how to get famous film actresses to stop molesting them.

After the team was featured in the star-studded inheritance film farce *The Wrong Box* (1966), director Stanley Donen approached them to do a film on anything that they were interested in. They just happened to have a hilarious reworking of a Faust story.

In *Bedazzled*, Stanley Moon (Moore), a dull, pathetic, short-order cook at a Wimpy Burger Bar, is about to hang himself out of unrequited love for a desirable waitress named Margaret Spencer (dazzling comedienne Eleanor Bron) when the Prince of Darkness, a.k.a. George Spigot (Cook) intercedes to give Moon seven wishes in exchange for his immortal soul.

> "Oh yes, I've learned from my mistakes, and I'm sure I could repeat them exactly."
> —Peter Cook

As Sister Stanley Moon (Dudley Moore) ponders his predicament, the Prince of Darkness (Peter Cook) enjoys romping on a trampoline in Bedazzled (1967).

"I just love the taste of honey on a man's lips," says Miss Lillian Lust (Raquel Welch), one of the Seven Deadly Sins in Bedazzled (1967).

What transpires would have filled even Goethe with mirth. With each fantasized scenario that poor Stanley concocts for himself and his dove, he manages to leave a loophole that Spigot uses to spectacularly sabotage him. Stanley can only escape each new nightmarish situation by blowing a raspberry (Bronx cheer to us Yanks) to return to reality. Here are the white and Auguste clowns incarnate.

Each scene gives Moore and Bron diverse characters to play, and they do, flawlessly. As a brilliant thinker, Stanley verbally dazzles Margaret at the zoo (while primates happily fornicate in the background) but is unable to be anything but an intellectual git in communicating his own lust until he practically rapes her at his flat. In another try, as the nymphomaniacal wife to Stanley's fabulously wealthy lord, Margaret manages simultaneously to be both upper-crust and lower-grunge. As the homewrecking wife and the best friend of a saintly husband, Margaret and Stanley are much too tortured to consummate their cravings for each other. Stanley's last, and seemingly foolproof, bid for union with his heart's desire is too heretical to describe—let's just say that nuns and trampolines play a part.

Through this wonderful trip, the Devil (Cook) appears again and again in guises including an old-lady-victimizing eyewash salesman, a cross-wiring phone repairman, an Oxford don (Sir Domination), a blind beggar, and an almost catatonic pop singer named Drimble Wedge. Back home in reality, the Prince of Darkness' headquarters are in a strip club; everything about him is deliciously, cheerfully cheesy, even his relationship with the Almighty.

The Seven Deadly Sins are there, too. Anger is his bouncer. Sloth is his lawyer. Envy is his barber. And Miss Lillian Lust (Raquel Welch) is his southern manicurist, who has a seduction scene with Moore that would put Bo Derek to shame. (In fact, the original title that Pete 'n' Dud wanted for their screenplay was simply *Raquel Welch*. It seems they wanted to see "Peter Cook and Dudley Moore in *Raquel Welch*" on the theater marquee.)

Working for a percentage of the gross "so we could make millions" (the optimistic Moore) or "remain totally penniless" (the jaundiced Cook), Cook wrote much of the script, and Moore composed the music. Donen even let them participate in the editing. As a result, the tone is so gleefully biting that you need a rabies shot after seeing it. *Bedazzled* bedazzled critics and audiences, though it proved a bit sophisticated for some viewers. The tragedy is that this gem is the duo's only real film output. The experimental 1960s were over all too quickly. Writing their own screenplays was a rare privilege, and as Cook had a dislike for performing other people's words (though he did play an English butler in the early eighties sitcom *The Two of Us*), the final credits are the final credits.

By 1972, the duo was back on the boards with their wildly successful sequel to *Beyond the Fringe* called *Good Evening*. Cook became increasingly busy with running his own comedy club, publishing a satire magazine called *Private Eye*, and, unfortunately, drinking. Pete 'n' Dud split for good in 1977. Moore wanted to act in other people's scripts. Cook "generously" said of his friend's ambitions, "Perhaps if I had been born with a clubfoot and a height problem, I'd have been as desperate as Dudley to become a star." But Moore did become a star, giving one of the best comic performances ever as a drunken millionaire in *Arthur* (1981). Cook died at the age of fifty-seven, and the world lost a brilliant comedian.

Python Power

And now for something completely different. If there were a team scepter for Pete 'n' Dud to pass on, it would have had to have been broken into pieces and divided among Eric Idle, John Cleese, Terry Jones, Graham Chapman, Terry Gilliam, and Michael Palin. These sultans of silliness became so synonymous with comedy at its best throughout the seventies and eighties that a whole generation of baby-boomers can still launch into one of their many sketches, with little or no provocation—and with little inclination to stop once they've started.

> *We've got to maintain a certain level of offense; otherwise we're just entertainment.*
> **—Terry Gilliam**

Though Terry Gilliam (director of *Brazil*, 1985, and *The Fisher King*, 1991) is quoted as saying, "I think it was John's homosexual love for Michael Palin that brought them together," the truth is a little more platonic. They all met in the collegiate playpen, of course—Idle, Cleese, and Chapman at Oxford, and Palin and Jones at Cambridge. Upon graduating, Palin, Idle, Chapman, and Cleese got jobs writing for Britain's archly funny interviewing icon, David Frost. Palin, Jones, Idle, and Gilliam also began writing for the television series *Do Not Adjust Your Set*. By mid-1969, a late-night time slot had opened up at the BBC, so the six joined forces to record thirteen half-hour comedy shows with no storyline whatsoever, which made the BBC sweat more than a little. The rest is hysteria. A cult audience grew, three more seasons followed, and by 1974 *Monty Python's Flying Circus* was soaring in syndication on America's PBS. The sheer wealth of their material was amazing, from The Ministry of Funny Walks to Dennis Moore, the lupine-stealing bandit. For all their variety and diversity, there was some consistency: Chapman more often than not appeared either in drag or as a bullish military man. Palin mastered the loonily cretinous characters. Cleese perfected irrationality and invective. Idle was the deranged blowhard, newscaster, or sleazebag. Jones' shrieking, elderly matrons became as inspired as his growing attention to directing. And Gilliam's visionary, lewdly Victorian, anatomical, political animations glued it all together.

They put the best of these skits into *And Now for Something Completely Different* (1972), taking potshots at everything from lumberjacks to a competition for Upper-Class Twit of the Year. They took Arthurian romance for a bumpy ride with *Monty Python and the Holy Grail* (1974), which included killer bunnies, coconuts, and knights who love a fight even when their arms and legs have been hacked off. In 1979, they decided to tackle a genre even more sacred than knighthood—the Good Book itself—and embarked on their greatest team effort, *The Life of Brian* (1979).

FROM LEFT TO RIGHT: Sir Lancelot (John Cleese), King Arthur (Graham Chapman), Sir Bedevere (Terry Jones), and Sir Galahad (Michael Palin) indulge in a little medieval mockery during Monty Python and the Holy Grail *(1974).*

Season's Greetings from Monty Python, the most successful comedy team in the world (except possibly for some other comedy teams, but we are English so perhaps we are the most successful English comedy team in the world. Well, damn it, our TV shows have been seen in 25 countries and our last movie did $9,000,000 distributor's gross, whatever that means, and we've sold a million and a quarter of our books and over a million copies of our record albums, so we're not exactly broke). Anyway, the point is we're back together again in 1978 for...MONTY PYTHON'S NEW FILM!
—January 4, 1978, ad in Variety *for Monty Python's new movie, at that point untitled*

The Goy Next Door

England's leading literary figure, H.G. Wells, once posited that if Jesus Christ had been hanged instead of crucified, Christianity's symbol might well be a noose. With that kind of logic, it's not unnatural to make a film about the boy next door to the Bethlehem manger who, somehow having been mistaken for a prophet through a series of mishaps, finds himself over his head in a world of daffy Judeo-Roman, political, personal, and religious intrigue. And that's the toned-down version.

Eric Idle claims that he was either in a bar in Amsterdam or a Chinese restaurant in London when the title for a film presented itself in his mind: *Jesus Christ—Lust for Glory*. Idle brought his naughty notion back to the boys and, as he admitted, "Naturally we started out with some awful jokes, how Jesus was really a terrible carpenter who kept hammering nails through his hands." After they got the Jesus-falling-off-his-donkey and the making-reservations-for-the-Last-Supper gags out of their systems, the Pythons had a change of heart. No research slouches, they had been plumbing the New Testament and other sources for information on Christ, and they decided he was much too good a bloke to be ridiculed. Instead, they targeted the boy next door, the Jews, the Roman Empire, and religion itself.

With this kind of following, who needs enemies? A few of the faithful from Monty Python's iconoclastic The Life of Brian (1979).

From the torridly inappropriate belt of its Shirley Bassey–esque (of James Bond film-theme fame) theme song, *The Life of Brian* is never anything less than outrageous. The three Magi, who mistakenly come not to the manger but to the home next door to explain that they were led by a star, are rebuffed by Brian's salty mother, Mandy (Terry Jones): "Led by a bottle is more like it." Years later, when the real Christ is preaching his Sermon on the Mount, the fun continues as Mandy and her mama's boy, Brian (Graham Chapman), join a crowd that is so far from the speaker that they completely misinterpret many of Christ's weighty words. Blessed are the cheesemakers? The Greek shall inherit the earth?

They buy rocks from a vendor for the stoning of a man accused of saying "Jehovah." The stoners, though they're supposed to be male, are all bloodthirsty, local housewives in drag who turn a respectable stoning into supermarket mayhem for the centurion in charge (John Cleese), who is crushed with a boulder. A little later, a former leper (Michael Palin) bends Brian's ear, saying that Christ cured him and robbed him of his livelihood. Brian attends a kiddie matinee at the Coliseum and gets embroiled with the constantly squabbling People's Front of Judea (not to be confused with the despicable counter-faction, the People's Judaic Front). Brian's test for entry to the group is the dangerous assignment of painting "Romans Go Home" in latin in the town square, but when the centurion catches him, he receives not death but a harsh grammar lesson (from John Cleese) and has to write his phrase correctly one thousand times all over the square. He gets involved in a botched

plot to kidnap Pontius Pilate's wife. Pilate (Michael Palin) sounds like Elmer Fudd and talks about his "very gweat fwend named Biggus Dickus," as all his guards snigger.

In his increasingly frantic efforts to escape the insanity he's entered, Brian poses among a group of false prophets, and because he can't think of anything to say, he is worshiped by the Messiah-hungry mob. Now, the real madness begins. Brian's road to martyrdom is paved with brilliant characters from the whole Python crew. Palin has another gem as a benevolent centurion cheerfully and compassionately leading prisoners off to crucifixion. Idle plays a Jewish merchant who refuses to sell Brian a gourd without haggling for it. Jones plays a naked holy man who breaks seventeen years of silence when Brian steps on his foot. And the scene where Brian awakens naked after a night of love with Judith Iscariot (someone's sister) and opens his window to find a huge, perfectly synchronized crowd of the faithful awaiting him ("There's no Messiah here! A mess, yes, but no Messiah!") is priceless.

The scene itself, shot in Monastir, Tunisia (as was *Star Wars*, 1977), employed five hundred Tunisian extras who didn't speak English. To get them all to lie down laughing, director Terry Jones originally had a Tunisian comic come in and tell jokes. When that didn't work, he communicated that he wanted them to do exactly as he did—and he promptly lay on the ground, kicking his legs up into the air.

All this mirth at organized religion's expense was lost on the producers at EMI, who pulled out of the Python project early on for fear of charges of anti-Semitism. (Some of those fears may have been justified, as the original script included a scene where Brian meets Otto, the leader of a Jewish resistance group who wants to create a Jewish state to last for one thousand years.)

HEY, WHAT'S THE BIG IDEA?

You're the junior vice president of Worldwide Motion Pictures (the largest production company on the planet). Believe it or not, your boss' (some suit from back east) impersonation of a creative idea was to split up every successful film comedy team that ever lived, and try some fresh combinations. Skeets Gallagher is hoofing it with Bob Hope, and Lou Costello is doing "Who's on First?" with Cheech Marin. The board of directors is less than pleased. To make things right, and to get your boss' job, untangle these misfit matches and place them in the right movies (the movie is always right for at least one of the partners). Their fathers thank you. Their mothers thank you. And they thank you.

PARTNER 1	PARTNER 2	MOVIE
1) Dan Rowan	A) Fibber McGee	a) The Maltese Bippy *(1969)*
2) Paul McCullough	B) Jerry Lewis	b) My Friend Irma *(1949)*
3) Jack Lemmon	C) Thomas Chong	c) The Odd Couple *(1968)*
4) Gene Wilder	D) Woolsey	d) Diplomaniacs *(1933)*
5) George Burns	E) Mike Myers	e) Here Comes Cookie *(1935)*
6) Larry Feinberg	F) Peter Marshall	f) Swingin' Along *(1962)*
7) Alfalfa Switzer	G) Huntz Hall	g) General Spanky *(1936)*
8) Mickey Rooney	H) John Sigvard Olsen	h) Fifty Million Frenchmen *(1931)*
9) Al Ritz	I) Gracie Allen	i) One in a Million *(1937)*
10) Bing Crosby	J) Donald O'Connor	j) Francis Goes to West Point *(1952)*
11) Charley McCarthy	K) George Moran	k) The Muppet Movie *(1979)*
12) Thelma Todd	L) Marjorie Main	l) Ma and Pa Kettle at Waikiki *(1955)*
13) Baby LeRoy	M) Eddie "Rochester" Anderson	m) It's a Gift *(1934)*
14) Woody Allen	N) Dan Aykroyd	n) Manhattan *(1979)*
15) Jack Benny	O) Edgar Bergen	o) Buck Benny Rides Again *(1940)*
16) John Belushi	P) W.C. Fields	p) Neighbors *(1981)*
17) Percy Kilbride	Q) Moses Harry Horowitz	q) Disorder in the Court *(1936)*
18) Dana Carvey	R) Darla Hood	r) Wayne's World *(1992)*
19) Cheech Marin	S) Dick Martin	s) Up in Smoke *(1978)*
20) Harold Ogden Johnson	T) Richard Pryor	t) The Silver Streak *(1976)*
21) Francis the Talking Mule	U) ZaSu Pitts	u) War Mamas *(1931)*
22) Leo Gorcey	V) Jimmy Ritz	v) Bowery Battalion *(1951)*
23) Tommy Noonan	W) Judy Garland	w) Babes in Arms *(1939)*
24) Charles Mack	X) Diane Keaton	x) A Nag in the Bag *(1938)*
25) Bert Wheeler	Y) Bob Hope	y) Road to Rio *(1947)*
26) Molly	Z) Walter Matthau	z) This Way Please *(1938)*
	AA) Robert Edwin Clark	aa) Odor in the Court *(1934)*

Luckily for the Python team, Eric Idle's old pal, former Beatle and budding film producer George Harrison, guaranteed the film's $4.5 million budget, putting up much of his publishing rights and mortgages as security (he claimed that watching Monty Python had helped him through his band's breakup). Even so, this fantastic film took almost as many hits as Martin Scorsese's *The Last Temptation of Christ* (1988). Not only did Senator Strom Thurmond force its closure in Columbia, South Carolina, theaters, but the Roman Catholic Archdiocese of New York denounced it, as did the Lutheran Council, and three rabbinical organizations called it a "crime against religion." But as Graham Chapman said, "Don't they realize that God has a sense of humor?"

Chapter Three

CHEMISTRY CLASS

Don't you ever let a woman grieve you,
just 'cause she's got that weddin' ring.
She'll love you and deceive you,
then she'll take your clothes and leave you,
'cause a woman is a sometime thing.

—Ira Gershwin, "A Woman Is a Sometime Thing"

Lucy Warriner (Irene Dunne) is trying to get rid of a little incriminating evidence before husband Jerry (Cary Grant) finds out, but Mr. Smith (Asta) isn't cooperating in The Awful Truth *(1937).*

It's an old formula for delightful disaster: a pair of itty-bitty XX chromosomes introduced to a pair of inky-dinky XY chromosomes, and...pow! Whether there is anything deeply, soulfully, intrinsically different about the sexes (anatomy notwithstanding) may remain a subject for debate, but there's no arguing that friction between these polar opposites has often heated up everything around them. In movies, this feisty stuff can get pretty interesting.

And when the amorous combat on the big screen is bitingly funny yet has a happy ending for man and woman, it's even better. Hollywood has long been mining this heterogenous gold with combatively diverse couples: Jimmy Cagney and Joan Blondell in *Sinner's Holiday* (1930), Rock Hudson and Doris Day in *Pillow Talk* (1959), Sir Laurence Olivier and Marilyn Monroe in *The Prince and The Showgirl* (1957), Dudley Moore and Liza Minelli in *Arthur* (1981), Meg Ryan and Tom Hanks in *Sleepless in Seattle* (1993), and Ted Danson and Whoopi Goldberg in *Made in America* (1993). The years have taken their toll, and now love is completely laughable. But who would want it any other way?

The Grip and the Slip

The real heyday for comedic couples, and certainly one of the shining moments for film funniness, began in the 1930s with a chaotic twist on romance called the screwball comedy. This hysterical hybrid reversed, jumbled, and otherwise toyed with power positions between classes and sexes and razzed the hell out of the sanctified stature of marriage, divorce, wealth, patriotism, intellectualism, and other icons of the era. Yet this rebellion against regular romance sprang from a pretty tight time.

Reeling from the 1929 stock market crash and staggering its way through the first years of the Great Depression, Hollywood felt morally chastened, as did much of America, for its wild youth of the twenties. The righteous call to Tinseltown to clean up its act—straight from Will Hays' Motion Picture Association of America—was answered by a 1930 production code that swore such oaths as "No picture shall be produced which will lower the moral standards of those who see it."

Just as studios were tempted to slip in more explicit violence and sexuality to lure Depression-era audiences to the movies, bigwigs started scrutinizing the Hollywood product for nudity, profanity, crime, and appropriate costuming. Hays made doubly sure they did so with the 1934 Production Code Administration, watchdogged by enemy-to-almost-everything (except good taste) Joseph L. Breen. The seal of approval from the Breen office could make or break most any picture.

In response to the crackdown, the early thirties saw the rise and sighing swell of "the weeper," moralistic tales of fallen women

that alluded to lots of nice naughtiness while emphasizing the terrible penalty paid for it, and in which nearly every up-and-coming female star had to do time. Yet, ever since the early twenties, German director Ernst Lubitsch had been quietly making merry, sophisticated comedies that hid his preoccupation with sex and money from the censors by cloaking them in innuendo and sparkling dialogue. Films such as *Trouble in Paradise* (1932) soon had all kinds of directors thinking about the man-woman thing as a vehicle for their own themes.

For socially conscious directors like Frank Capra, the man-woman thing could also pit haves against have-nots and keep it sweetly funny—so much so that the films would be dubbed Capracorn—whatever the proletarian message. Veteran physical comedy master Leo McCarey could retain some of the knockabout nonsense and bizarre characters that were rapidly losing vogue, with stories of the eccentric rich, who could behave any way they wanted (especially when in love). Artistically inclined types such as Gregory LaCava didn't have to sacrifice style while tackling stories of gritty substance. Seasoned gangster-picture maker Howard Hawks could launch comedy into overdrive with dialogue as rapid-fire as his tommy-guns in *The Criminal Code* (1931).

For the studios, comedy's turn to fractious romance was just as big a boon. When the chemistry between two stars was just right, the studios' ironclad contracts ensured their ability to pair the stars in vehicle after vehicle—whether they wanted to be paired or not. You just never knew how a screwball was going to come at you. The same year baseball pitcher supreme Carl Hubbell downed batting greats with his varied "screwball" at the 1934 All-Star Game, Frank Capra threw one of the first screwballs into the cinematic ballpark—a ball no one wanted, not even the actors—and made history with a story about a bus ride. But what a ride it was: a hard-bitten reporter, a runaway bride...and the rest is chemistry!

The Road Picture Nobody Wanted to Make... but Were Glad They Did!

Frank Capra had lived a full life by the age of thirty-six. His Sicilian farm family had been destitute upon its arrival in America, and he had worked his way through high school by hawking newspapers in downtown Los Angeles. After college at Cal Tech in chemical engineering, he had gone off to fight in WWI, contracted influenza, and returned later than most GIs—to find jobs especially scarce. Riding the rails between supporting himself doing everything from hustling poker to tutoring the son of a gold-mine owner, he got his first taste of film directing with an eccentric, aging actor in *Fultah Fisher's Boarding House* (1922). The film bug bit.

Jobs as a film editor, a prop man, and finally as a gag man for the Mack Sennett and Hal Roach studios during the silent era cul-

minated in Capra's directing (and cowriting) silent star Harry Langdon's first three films, in 1926 and 1927. When Langdon fired Capra to take over the directing duties himself, the childlike comedian's career plummeted. Capra's, however, had picked up. In 1928, Hollywood's "poverty row" studio, Columbia Pictures, had hired Capra at $1,000 a picture. (In return for such a small sum, he had complete creative control over his projects.) By the summer of 1933, Capra was living the good life. He had easily survived the movies' transition to sound and was largely keeping his studio afloat with minor hits like *That Certain Thing* (1928), *Platinum Blonde* (1931), and *American Madness* (1932).

Capra was vacationing in the well-known watering hole of Palm Springs, California, and working with his script collaborator, Robert Riskin, on the story for the 1933 weeper *Lady for a Day* when he picked up the August issue of *Cosmopolitan* while waiting for a haircut in a barber shop. In it was a short piece, "Night Bus," by Samuel Hopkins Adams, about a wrangling romance between a spoiled, fugitive heiress named Ellen Andrews and a bohemian painter named Peter Warne during a long bus ride. Capra liked it, as did Riskin, and discovered that his relatively impoverished studio could get it for "buttons" ($5,000 to us).

Selling it to Columbia mogul Harry Cohn was another story. But as Capra said, "Uncertainty is the fun of it all; the door that can't

> *People found the film longer than usual and, surprise, funnier, much funnier than usual. But the biggest surprise of all, they could remember in detail a good deal of what went on in the film and they found that everybody else did and that it was great fun talking about this and that scene, and, "Let's go see it again and take the Johnsons." The quietness burst into a proverbial prairie fire.*
> —Frank Capra, on
> *It Happened One Night* (1934)

Fed up with waiting for a ride, Claudette Colbert will show Clark Gable that limb is mightier than thumb in It Happened One Night *(1934).*

be locked by film Rajahs against adventuresome newcomers." Cohn, a hardcase if there ever was one, balked. Bus pictures, two of which had recently been released, were poison, he said. When Capra protested, Cohn barked, "Listen, fat head, Irving Thalberg has offered me a $50,000 bonus and the loan of one of his stars if you make a picture for him."

Capra was hamstrung by his contract. He dutifully journeyed to MGM to make *Soviet* with Wallace Beery, Marie Dressler, Joan Crawford, and a hard-bitten player of gangsters and he-men named Clark Gable. When Thalberg's health failed, MGM vice president Louis B. Mayer, eager to sabotage any plan of Thalberg's, scrapped the picture. Back at Columbia, Capra insisted once again on making "Night Bus," and when he said he was heading back to Palm Springs to write the script, Cohn relented: "Go where the hell-ever you want. But get that word bus out of the title. It's poison!"

Capra and Riskin wrote away on *It Happened One Night* (1934)—with no mention of the word "bus"—annoying their poolside neighbors by laughing at their own jokes. Then they went shopping for a leading lady. They first brought the script to Myrna Loy (of later Thin Man movies fame). No dice. Fresh-faced Margaret Sullivan,

A pensive moment for America's best-loved director of comedies with a conscience, Frank Capra.

of later *The Moon's Our Home* (1936) fame, also nixed it. Miriam Hopkins (later the star of *The Richest Girl in the World*, 1934), wouldn't go near it. Constance Bennett, who would go on to make *Topper* (1937), would only say yes if she could buy the script outright and rewrite it.

Baffled, the duo called upon their pal, writer Myles Connolly, to eyeball their story for its weaknesses. Connolly came up with two brainstorms: one, that Ellie, the heiress, is not "a brat because she's an heiress, but because she's bored with being an heiress." And two, that Peter, instead of being a "long-haired, flowing-tied Greenwich Village painter," become a man's man and a newspaper reporter, preferably one who had a certain interest in covering the heiress' escapade during their bus sojourn from Miami to New York City. The rewrite took only a week. Around this time, Harry Cohn got a call from Louis B. Mayer, who wanted to make good on MGM's promise to send over a star, and it seemed that Clark Gable had had the audacity to ask for more money. "I've got an actor who's been a bad boy," Mayer confided, "and I'd like to spank him." Sending Gable (who had never done comedy) to the Siberia of Columbia was an offer that Cohn couldn't refuse. (Gable did come down to visit Capra's office, albeit drunk, surly, and arrogant. On his way out of the building, he yelled to the office staff, "Hey you guys! Why ain't you wearin' parkas in Siberia?" But he took the script with him.)

Armed with a leading man, in a last-ditch effort to get a reputable leading lady, Capra paid a personal visit on French-born actress Claudette Colbert. He hadn't forgotten that he had directed her in the modest flop *For the Love of Mike* only six years earlier. She was busily packing for a vacation when he arrived, but the director persisted. Colbert, less than eager, fliply asked for double her normal fee of $25,000 a picture and stipulated that the film had to be finished in four weeks so that she could go off to visit friends in Sun Valley, Idaho, for Christmas. Capra agreed. Here was a demanding, spoiled, talented woman so much like his heiress, Ellie Andrews, that he could tailor the role to fit her.

With so little time, Capra shot his scenes fast and loose. Scenes like the spontaneous group sing-along on the bus were almost completely improvised, with Capra rushing out for extra cameras to record the group spirit. In another bus scene, where the newspaper hound's sleeve button gets caught up in the heiress' dress, Capra let the cameras run again and record the fluster of veritable strangers.

Capra had reason to laugh, but the high-strung Colbert fussed on the set. One of the most notable instances occurred during the famous scene where Ellie and Peter are reduced to hitchhiking. After a manly display of hitching techniques from Gable, Colbert was supposed to prove once and for all that "the limb is mightier than the thumb." There was a modesty problem, however. Colbert vehemently resisted undressing in front of the camera, let alone Gable, and she wasn't about to expose her shapely gams on the road in broad daylight. In desperation, Capra finally had a chorus girl come in to double, and only when Colbert got a gander at the pudgy legs about to be immortalized as her own did she hoist her skirt.

Gable, on the other hand, had gotten over his initial sulks and threw himself into the picture, and in preparation he had even ridden a night bus from Los Angeles to San Francisco, fraternizing all the way, his disguise an old hat pulled down over his face. On the set, his chemistry with the mercurial Colbert was amazing: she both irritated and bewitched her costar. As Capra said, "All she had to do was bug Gable on camera as much as she bugged me off camera." As frosty as she was in her "brat" scenes at the beginning, her Ellie was increasingly game during the famed doughnut-dunking lesson and hilarious fishwife charade in the tourist cabin, and proved equally steamy in her cabin bedtime scenes with Gable.

Gable did some steaming of his own—smoking in the dark and staring at the flimsy curtain that divided him from his new motel cabinmate. When Peter warns Ellie to remove her draped undergarments from across the walls of Jericho—a blanket hung across a rope—it's not neatness talking. His garrulously narrated undressing scene (sans undershirt) in front of Colbert before they bed down for the night—the only scene Capra had to reshoot because Colbert didn't look scared enough—resulted in a 50 percent drop in nationwide undershirt sales within a year.

Peter and Ellie's screwball journey was so funny, so subtly sexually charged, so socially timely, and so believable for all its snappy dialogue, right down to its screwy ending, that after four weeks of shooting and a $325,000 budget, Capra knew he had a masterpiece. *It Happened One Night* not only became the prairie fire that Capra desired, it also made history, sweeping an unprecedented five Oscars that year for Best Actor, Best Actress, Best Writing, Best Director, and Best Picture.

Capra, whom mighty MGM had rejected, passed out on his lawn on Oscar night with his trophy in his hand, having cemented a golden reputation and having delivered his poverty-row studio into the big leagues. Colbert rocketed to screwball superstardom (even though she reportedly said to a friend after filming, "I've just finished the worst picture in the world"). And Gable, the bad boy who was going to be punished for asking for a raise, returned to MGM as their reigning male star—at three times his former salary. The last laugh was on Louis B. Mayer.

The Screwball Fireball and Love in the Asylum

The woman to whom Clark Gable lost his heart in real life—she had the nerve to call him Pappy—the woman who was a flower of a frail feminine loveliness, yet sharp as a tack and headstrong as a whirlwind; the woman who may have been the queen of screwball comedy, went into the movie business shortly after being voted Queen of the May when she was a sixteen-year-old student at Hollywood's Fairfax High School. Carole Lombard started early, but she had a long and bumpy road to stardom.

A silent-film contract at Mack Sennett's studio as a bathing beauty led Lombard to the Pathé Studio's talkies, but she was dropped when Constance Bennett didn't want another blonde on the roster as competition. Though a car accident in the mid-1920s made her "less desirable" because of a small scar on her cheek, Lombard eventually wound up with a seven-year, $375-a-week contract at Paramount, where she was developed for the weepers as the tragic yet mysterious "orchid lady." The orchid soon withered—she stank at hoity-toity seriousness—but Lombard later flowered, as she married cool and composed costar William Powell in 1931 (though they would part amicably a year later).

What Powell and everyone else who came into contact with Lombard discovered was that, despite her classy and pristine looks, she was much more temperamentally suited for madcap comedy. She lived fast and loved to dance, and was a rabid tennis player, a chronic practical joker, a pal to grips and lighting technicians, a favorite line-reality-tester for comedy writers, and an expert in contract negotiations. At an early age (for protection in the sleazy world of Hollywood), she had her brothers teach her every conceivable foul, dirty, and obscene word they could come up with. They came up with many. Consequently, Lombard had a mouth like a sailor, and in Hollywood, land of ex–garment salesmen and cigar-smoking secretary-chasers, that was a good thing.

It's said that curmudgeon Harry Cohn once bluntly told her that she'd better ditch her platinum blonde hair because it made her look like a whore. Lombard acknowledged that if anyone would know what a whore looked like, it was Cohn, so she'd better take his advice. Cohn, who liked getting as good as he gave, took the scrappy starlet under his wing.

A couple of snakes in the grass, Fred MacMurray and Carole Lombard, give each other the once-over in **Hands Across the Table** *(1935).*

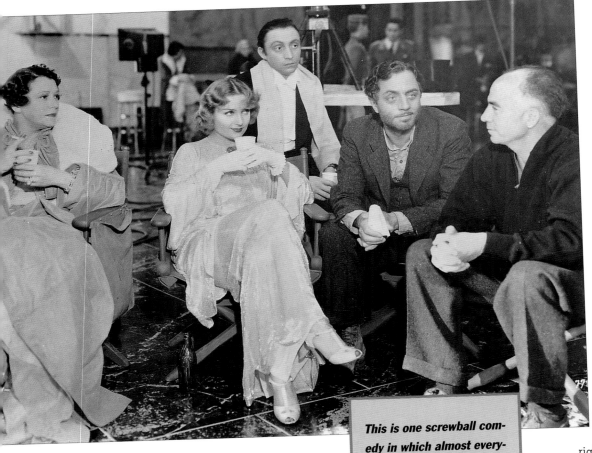

Her big break came when Cohn secured her the lead in the father of screwball comedy, Howard Hawks' film of Ben Hecht and Charles MacArthur's seminal 1932 stage play, *The Twentieth Century* (1934). Here, for perhaps the first time, glittering and urbane dialogue and slapstick physicality would be slammed together in zany overdrive to make heads—and some stomachs—spin.

The former matinee idol, current ham, and sometimes brilliant actor John Barrymore had long been slated to star as Oscar Jaffe, a theatrical impresario so egomaniacal, overbearing, and crazily charismatic that only Barrymore would do. But who wanted to play across from this titan? The search began for the actress to portray Lily Garland, the renegade diva whom Jaffe long ago discovered as plain Mildred Plotka and whom he now finds himself confronting on a speeding locomotive from Chicago to New York. Ina Claire, Tallulah Bankhead, and five other actresses had all refused billing with the notoriously drunken, lecherous Barrymore. Hawks wanted Miriam Hopkins, but Cohn suggested Lombard, to whom Hawks was coincidentally related. As Hawks remembered, "She was a second cousin of mine and an amazing personality.... I told her if she acted, I'd fire her. And she said, 'Okay, I'll do anything that comes into my head.' I said, 'That's what I want you to do.' She would just throw lines at him [Barrymore] so fast that he didn't know what to do sometimes. It was so fast, I didn't understand it part of the time."

By the time Lily's squabbling, high-speed romance with Oscar had reached its cynical terminus, Lombard was a hot Hollywood property. Her reputation as a comedy wildcat was even stronger after a role as a gold-digging manicurist in *Hands Across the Table*

> *This is one screwball comedy in which almost everyone seems genuinely crazy—not nutty, not naughty, not even screwy, but really insane.*
> —Richard Corliss, on *My Man Godfrey* (1936)

(1935) with a sleazy Fred MacMurray. Her witty former husband, Powell, who had already become a screwball staple himself with slinky Myrna Loy in director W. S. Van Dyke's Thin Man detective film series, had little trouble wangling his ex to star opposite him in one of the classiest—and most class-conscious—screwballs ever, *My Man Godfrey* (1936).

New Universal Studios head Charles M. Rogers had bought the rights to writer Eric Hatch's story "Irene the Stubborn Girl," which had been serialized in the May and June 1935 issues of *Liberty Magazine*. The tale followed the escapade of a dim young deb named Irene Bullock who finds a "forgotten man" (a bum to us) at New York's city dump and pays him $5 to be an item for a society scavenger hunt. She then hires him on as a butler to her rich family of spoiled eccentrics. This is when the real fun starts: Godfrey is a down-on-his-luck Boston blueblood and just the man to whip Irene's flaky family into shape. Keeping from falling in love with his young charge is something else.

The chemistry between Powell and Lombard is as palpable as was that between Gable and Colbert. Powell's composed and continental cool, in contrast with Lombard's lightheaded, lithesome, libidinous little-girl-lostness is as arousing as it is surprisingly unsentimental. Lombard gives the dizzy blonde a whole new persona: she's not dumb—she's breathless, spoiled, self-assured, and sincerely insane.

To make matters merrier, Irene's unclear nuclear family are consummate character actors, down to the clan "protégé" (that's gigolo to us), Carlo (Mischa Auer), who, when he's not mooching, gives one of the best gorilla imitations ever seen, in an effort to revive Irene from one of her many faints. Butter wouldn't melt in the mouth of Irene's big sister, Cornelia (former Harvard College dean of women Gail Patrick). Her mother (Alice Brady) is the perfect blend of dithering and darling: she sees pixies on her bed to accompany her hangovers—to which Godfrey serves her a hair of the dog, saying, "There's nothing like a little counter-irritant in the morning." As the gravel-voiced paterfamilias, Alexander Bullock (former jockey Eugene Pallette) sums it all up as he croaks, "All you need to start an asylum is an empty room and the right kind of people."

OOOH, WHY DON'T YA COME UP AND QUOTE ME SOMETIME

As chemistry goes, Brooklyn's own Mary Jane (a.k.a. Mae) West was in a class by herself. In fact, she was a one-woman graduate seminar in biomechanics. The daughter of a heavyweight prize-fighter, a child actress by the age of six, and originator of the "shimmy dance," she became the most successful and most imitated film comedienne who had ever lived. Yet for all her eye-rolling, hip-swinging, overripe sexuality, Mae had a way with words as well. She wrote the lion's share of her film dialogue, but then, she'd had practice.

As early as 1926, she was the tantalizing toast of New York, when Sex, the Broadway play she had written, produced, and directed, was closed by the cops and she was jailed for ten days (though the warden did take her out to dinner every night). This mistress of sexual innuendo wasn't afraid to deal with interracial sexuality, homosexuality, or any kind of sexuality in her plays. By the time she came to Paramount, she had guts enough to ask how much studio head Adolf Zukor made. When told that he made $250,000 a year, she asked for $251,000—and had clout enough to get it, along with the power to rewrite her own dialogue.

Though the Hays office would clamp down on her lascivities, the then-highest-paid woman in America always beat them with her untouchable double entendres. She was influential in bringing African-American performers into films. She only showed her legs in one film, I'm No Angel (1933). And whether paired with the steely George Raft in Night After Night (1932), the suave Cary Grant in She Done Him Wrong (1933), or the great W.C. Fields in My Little Chickadee (1940), she always held her own. And here's Mae on...

> In this picture, Mae West stole everything but the cameras.
> —George Raft, on Mae West's first film

QUALITY	"A hard man is good to find."
HEIGHT	"Let's forget about the 6 feet (1.8m) and talk about the 7 inches (17.8cm)."
MATH	"A man has one hundred dollars and you leave with two—that's subtraction."
KNOWLEDGE	"Baby, I went to night school."
SIN	"To err is human but it feels divine."
IMAGE	"It's better to be looked over than overlooked."
PURITY	"I used to be Snow White, but I drifted."
SIZE	"That myth about big noses don't hold true. Otherwise, Jimmy Durante would have been the biggest lover in Hollywood."
ERNST LUBITSCH	"We called him son-of-Lubitsch behind his back."
GEORGE CUKOR	"George Cukor and I are friends. We never worked together."
MARRIAGE	"Marriage is like a book. The whole story takes place between covers."
SELECTION	"It's not the men in my life that counts—it's the life in my men."
MALE EGO	"Whenever a guy starts boasting about his family tree, I seem to smell a strong sniff of sap rising."
WELCOMES	"Is that a pistol in your pocket or are you just glad to see me?"
SCANDAL	"Women with pasts interest men because men hope that history will repeat itself."
CLASS	"Gentlemen may prefer blondes, but who says that blondes prefer gentlemen?"
TIMING	"He who hesitates is last."
INTELLIGENCE	"Brains are an asset to the woman in love who's smart enough to hide them."
FAIRNESS	"All discarded lovers should be given a second chance, but with somebody else."
PASTIMES	"Men are my hobby. If I ever got married, I'd have to give it up."
SEX	"The sexiest thing in the world is to be totally naked with your wedding band on."

The right kind of person was at the helm of this fine film. Gregory LaCava—a moody, fight-prone, independent director. He was a drinking buddy of W.C. Fields who kept an open bar on the *Godfrey* set and was an early Tinseltown devotee of psychiatry—he knew both sides of the social register, and how. As a kid in Pennsylvania, he left boxing to study at the Art Institute of Chicago. As a cartoonist for the *New York World*, he befriended the macho likes of Damon Runyon, Grantland Rice, and Jack Dempsey. After marrying artist, feminist, and socialist Beryl Morse, he kept up his painting with New York's gritty Ashcan school, while making the move from animation (he was the first to put the "Katzenjammer Kids" comic strip onto film) to live action. LaCava's keen sense of timing from his animation days is evident in *My Man Godfrey*'s peerless pace, and his aesthetics are reflected in the majestic opening credits, a musically accompanied panorama of a New York nighttime skyline with every cast and crew member's credit up in neon lights.

Lombard was a sensation and went on to costar in celebrated screwballs: as a scheming young thing with Frederic March in William Wellman's *Nothing Sacred* (1937), an embattled newlywed with Jimmy Stewart in *Made for Each Other* (1939), a woman momentarily unmarried to Robert Montgomery in Alfred Hitchcock's contribution to the genre, *Mr. and Mrs. Smith* (1941), and Jack Benny's costar in the classic Lubitsch satire *To Be or Not To Be* (1942). When World War II became a national concern, Lombard threw all her energies into helping the war effort; it cost her and

movie audiences dearly. In 1942, while flying back to Hollywood from a nationwide bond drive, her plane went down outside Las Vegas, Nevada. Screwball—and her heartbroken husband, Clark Gable—were never the same.

Judy, Judy, Judy!

The undisputed king of screwball was, of course, Cary Grant. No other male star made more memorable comedies, looked as handsome, had better timing, or claimed a throwaway style more often imitated (even by Tony Curtis to woo Marilyn Monroe in Billy Wilder's *Some Like It Hot*, 1959). No other screen celebrity brought in such consistent box-office bucks from the mid-thirties all the way through the mid-sixties.

Grant was born into extreme poverty in Bristol, England, and only escaped it when, as a teenager, he joined an acrobatic troupe that traveled to the United States in 1920. Tumbling out of the show to give vaudeville a try with a mind-reader act, he bit the dust, returning to England three years later. By the early 1930s, Grant had broken in as a stage actor back home and decided to give Hollywood a go. His job at Paramount as a reader to starlets who were making screen tests got him an acting contract for $450 a week. After playing a heavy to Marlene Dietrich's siren in *Blonde Venus* (1932), he fell into the grasp of the woman whom he credited with teaching him comedy.

Mae West plucked Grant from relative obscurity to play opposite her in both *She Done*

> *I often think my life has been a failure. But whenever I drop into a theater and hear women laughing at one of my films, I think well, if I brightened their day before they went home and did the dishes, maybe my life wasn't wasted after all.*
> —Cary Grant

Before he found his celebrated timing and sense of humor, Cary Grant was the perfect hunk to offset stars like Mae West (left) in I'm No Angel *(1933) and Marlene Dietrich (opposite) in* Blonde Venus *(1932).*

Him Wrong (1933) and *I'm No Angel* (1933), and by 1936, he had achieved stardom playing opposite Katherine Hepburn in *Sylvia Scarlett*. In 1937, he perfected the Cary Grant image of droll detachment in a film about the most delightfully dysfunctional divorce ever devised, with the help of a man who called himself "a bargain-basement Cary Grant."

The Humanist

> Leo McCarey understands people better than anyone else in Hollywood.
> —Jean Renoir, French filmmaker

Leo McCarey, like Cary Grant, was a long time in coming to his moment of truth. The son of a genteel Los Angeles fight promoter, he was a newsboy, as was Frank Capra. He later hustled himself through the University of Southern California's law school, set up a private-eye business, and even tried his hand at songwriting. (His only sell, "When the Eagle Flaps His Wings and Calls on the Kaiser," was released just before the WWI armistice. So much for timing.) After a shot in Hollywood as an assistant to horror director Todd Browning, Leo flopped with his own first feature, *Society Secrets* (1921). But the following six years with the Hal Roach Studios, where McCarey was a gag man, head of production, and finally a director, seasoned him for success. Not only did he eventually work with Laurel and Hardy as well with the Marx Brothers, but also with W.C. Fields, George Burns, Gracie Allen, Mae West, and even the great Charles Laughton, in *Ruggles of Red Gap* (1935).

> At comedy, no one was better than Leo McCarey.
> —Frank Capra

With his father's death in 1936 and his own near death from milk fever during the filming of Harold Lloyd's comeback film, *The Milky Way* (1936), he resolved that life was short enough that he only wanted to direct and produce comedies from then on. After a film at Paramount recounting the joys of marriage between two septuagenarians on the skids in *Make Way for Tomorrow* (1937), McCarey jumped ship to Columbia to take a loving look at divorce.

Ah, Marriage! Ah, Divorce!

> What pleases me the most about The Awful Truth *is that it told somewhat the story of my life. Don't repeat that—my wife will kill me.*
> —Leo McCarey

The Awful Truth (1937) is a down-and-dirty tale about a scandal-ridden (and unfaithful) society wife who needs her rakish (and unfaithful) ex-husband to clear her name so that she can profitably remarry. And while their marriage may have revolved around deception, their divorce could reveal the romantic spark that the ironic couple badly needs.

The original 1921 Broadway play finds an innocent and newly divorced Norman Satterly ensconced in a plush jail of a country club for husbands whose ex-wives are after their community property. In the 1937 screenplay for *The Awful Truth*, renamed protagonist Jerry Warriner (Cary Grant) has cooked his own goose when he comes back from a supposed two-week vacation in Florida to find that not only is his wife, Lucy (Irene Dunne), just getting back from an overnight with her smoldering vocal coach, but she calls his bluff when he gives her the Florida orange he sent—with a California stamp on it.

As the divorce progresses, the joint-custody squabble over a fox terrier named Mr. Smith keeps the separated spouses within sparring distance, and visitation rights give them a full view of each other's follies. Lucy gets so lonely that she takes up with a blockheaded Texas oilman named Daniel Leeson (a hilariously hick Ralph Bellamy), while Jerry plays around with cabaret singer Dixie Bell (Joyce Compton), whose rendition of "Gone With the Wind" blows her costume away bit by bit.

Naturally, they exploit each other's foibles mercilessly. The suave Jerry is tickled to pay a club orchestra to reprise a song just so his nondancing wife can get dragged around the dance floor one more time by her toe-squashing beau. The glittering Lucy is delighted to crash Jerry's attempt to marry an heiress, under the uncouth disguise of his slatternly sister. The jabs dizzily escalate along with the feeling that this wayward couple were made for each other—if they can ever find a way back through the mess they've made. With all the daggers flying, it's easy to believe that the script passed through the hands of seven writers (including Dorothy Parker) as well as McCarey himself. And by the time McCarey started shooting, the script he was satisfied with was scribbled on scraps of brown paper.

THAT NASTY PIANIST

The nimblest set of fingers, and one of the sharpest tongues that Hollywood ever claimed, belonged not to a movie star, mogul, or screenwriter but to a musician who played cynical sidekicks in thirteen movies, including Rhapsody in Blue *(1945)*, The Barkleys of Broadway *(1949)*, An American in Paris *(1951)*, and Band Wagon *(1953)*. Oscar Levant, the son of a watchmaker, wowed radio audiences as a musical prodigy on Information Please, *as he could identify almost any classical piece by name and composer after hearing just three bars. Later, as a pianist, his recording of George Gershwin's* Rhapsody in Blue *was Columbia Records' all-time best-selling album, and he became the highest-paid concert artist in America, outdoing Vladimir Horowitz and Arthur Rubinstein. As a composer, he had a mentor in Arnold Schoenberg and admirers like Aaron Copland.*

Yet Levant dropped both popular songwriting and classical composition because he felt that he would never be better than Gershwin and Copland. He became a barbiturate addict and was diagnosed as manic-depressive, and was the first celebrity to talk openly about drug withdrawal and mental illness on television. His biting humor on- and offscreen became legendary. Here's Oscar...

With wit as lancing as his music was lyrical, Oscar Levant (seated) keeps things edgy in An American in Paris (1951).

TO GRETA GARBO	*"Sorry, I didn't catch the name."*
ON FITNESS	*"My favorite exercises are groveling, brooding, and mulling."*
AMBITION	*"So little time, so little to do."*
EGO	*"An evening with George Gershwin is a George Gershwin evening."*
IMAGE	*"I'm a controversial figure. My friends either dislike me or hate me."*
ROMANCE	*"Madame, I'll memorize your name and then throw my head away."*
FAME	*"I play an unsympathetic part—myself."*
CIVIL RIGHTS	*"I'm for disintegration—personal disintegration."*
PURITY	*"I knew Doris Day before she became a virgin."*
ENTERTAINMENT	*"A musical is a series of catastrophes ending with a floor show."*
ATTIRE	*"I'm sorry, but my regular attire is white tie and straitjacket."*
TALENT	*"Talent is like a baby. Wrap it up in wool and it goes to sleep."*
SELF-PITY	*"It's the only pity that counts."*
MALE TALENT	*"Laurence Olivier is the most overrated actor on earth. Take away the wives and the looks and you have John Gielgud."*
FEMALE TALENT	*"If Ginger Rogers is an actress, so am I."*
PRIORITIES	*"I have to hang up now or I'll be too sleepy to take my sleeping pill."*
INTEGRITY	*"A lofty attitude assumed by someone who is unemployed."*
CHUTZPAH	*"That quality which enables a man who has murdered his mother and father to throw himself on the mercy of the court as an orphan."*
MARRIAGE	*"On one occasion when Judy Garland and I embraced each other, I felt it was such a unification of two great pill repositories that it must have been a peak in pharmaceutical history. If Judy and I had married she would have given birth to a sleeping pill instead of a child—we could have named it Barb Iturate."*
HIMSELF	*"There is a thin line between genius and insanity. I have erased that line."*

Even the first shot was winged. When the director discovered that Dunne was a bad amateur pianist and Bellamy a hound-dog singer, he immediately plunked them down at a piano and had them warble "Home on the Range." On other scenes, McCarey might provide an opening line like, "If it isn't my ex!" and let his actors take it from there. A nervous Grant at first offered to buy out his own contract for $5,000, but he eventually got into the swing of Leo's improvised style and was soon crafting some of his best throwaways, including, "The judge says it's my day to see the dog." He also came up with the idea of tickling Dunne with a pencil in a scene where he was hiding behind the door, listening to her make conversation with Bellamy.

This kind of teamwork made *The Awful Truth* awfully well received. It won LaCava an Oscar for Best Director. It refined the weirdly detached yet attractive persona of Cary Grant. It gave sexual stature to a mature Irene Dunne, herself fifteen years older than screwball actresses like Ginger Rogers. It even paid tribute to McCarey's past gags with the Roach Studios—Grant's hat trick carries a distinct note of Stan Laurel.

This is a hell of a way to keep a gal from retiring, points out reporter Rosalind Russell to her boss, Cary Grant, in His Girl Friday *(1940).*

> *I don't use funny lines. They're not funny unless you see them....They become funny because of their attitudes, because of the attitudes that work against what they're trying to say. And to me, that's the funniest comedy in the world.*
> **—Howard Hawks**

Overachiever Overdrive

If Cary Grant was the king of screwball, director Howard Hawks was its god. Well known for fine westerns such as *Red River* (1948) and *Rio Bravo* (1959), war movies such as *Sergeant York* (1941) and *Air Force* (1943), and dramas such as *To Have and Have Not* (1944), *Scarface* (1932), and *The Big Sleep* (1946), Hawks managed to direct some of screwball's most celebrated chemical explosions, including *His Girl Friday* (1940), *Ball of Fire* (1942), *I Was a Male War Bride* (1949), and *Monkey Business* (1952).

Hawks may have launched screwball into orbit with his histrionic, historic *The Twentieth Century* (1934), but he attained hyperspeed and, some say, perfection with the frenzy called *Bringing Up Baby* (1938). Put a brilliant, uptight, engaged paleontologist (Cary Grant), a love-hungry, harebrained heiress (Katherine Hepburn), a leopard named Baby (Nissa), and a fossil-stealing terrier named George (Asta) together, and the words "intercostal clavicle" may never sound the same. From virtually the first scene of Dudley Nichols' script—a serene game of golf—the pace becomes so breakneck, the funny lines and calamities come so fast and furiously, that you might want to consider an oxygen mask for the duration.

In creating his madness, Hawks reached back to another comic era. A tremendous fan of the silent clowns, he first convinced Grant to model Huxley, his upright, everything-happens-to-me scientist, on Harold Lloyd—right down to the glasses. As for the male-female component, he harked back to Buster Keaton's love-hate relationship with his bumbling belle in *The General* (1927).

There is a distinct feeling that blood might be shed as Huxley sinks deeper and deeper into the morass of heiress Susan's wacky world. Before the bone-smashing ending—the defining image of screwball comedy—he's reduced to throwing rocks at important people's windows, rending garments in restaurants, transporting tame leopards across state lines and mistakenly facing feral ones, falling into swamps, following little dogs around to help them dig holes in the dirt, landing in jail, and, in one of the many climaxes, forced into women's clothing in front of the one patroness who might fund his future, a situation that gave Grant one of his wildest throwaway explanations ever, as he replied, complete with balletic leap, "Oh, I don't know, I just turned gay all of a sudden!"

Indeed, the atmosphere on the set was gay. Hepburn served tea daily. Hawks took off entire days to take his cast to the horse races. Improv was everywhere, though getting Kate Hepburn to that point was a little tougher. *Bringing Up Baby* was her first all-out comedy, and at first she was a bit forced and too overtly comic, laughing at her own jokes like a bad Stan Laurel. Borrowing once again from the masters, Hawks explained Chaplin's assertion that comedy must be played seriously. She still didn't get it. Finally, he

ABOVE: A tale of two egos. John Barrymore and Carole Lombard were made for each other in Howard Hawks' Twentieth Century (1934). BELOW: The scientist, the debutante, and the leopard. Cary Grant and Katherine Hepburn are a little unsure of their compatibility in Bringing Up Baby (1938).

brought in veteran vaudevillian Walter Catlett to show Hepburn what he meant. Any lesser star would have fumed as Catlett enacted her scenes with Cary Grant, but the game Hepburn not only proved an apt pupil, she insisted that Catlett get the plum part of Constable Slocum. Soon Hepburn was riffing with her own gems, as when she was limping on casually after losing the heel to her shoe and quipping, "I was born on the side of a hill."

It was over the heads of many of its viewers and overbudget for its producers, and at its release Hepburn had just placed first on the Independent Theater Owners Association's list of box-office poison. Still, *Bringing Up Baby* eventually showed everyone just how far a screwball could go and still be a hit. Every successfully disastrous date-movie since—from the copycat *What's Up, Doc?* (1972) to Martin Scorsese's *After Hours* (1985) to Jonathan Demme's *Something Wild* (1986) to Blake Edwards' *Blind Date* (1987)—owes Hawks and company a screwy debt of thanks.

Closing the Circle

Preston Sturges wasn't like other directors. Playwright Alexander King dubbed him "the Toscanini of the pratfall." Movie star Joel McCrea admitted, after working on *The Palm Beach Story* (1942), that "I never worked with [a director] where I had so much fun. I really felt like I'd do it for nothing." Sturges hired a piano player to keep his cast entertained on the set, and without competitive paranoia, his sets were usually open for visitors. He strongly encouraged his cast and crew to view the dailies with him. (As William Demarest—Uncle Charley from TV's *My Three Sons*—once grumbled, "We always had to look at them every goddamn night. Then he'd start to put the picture together and you'd have to watch that, too!")

Like fellow whiz-kid Orson Welles, Sturges wrote some of his most acclaimed films (a very tough thing to get away with in Hollywood). And like Robert Altman, he established a permanent stable of comedic actors to work with, which included new blood as well as silent stars, such as the Keystone Kops' Chester Conklin. He is credited with pioneering today's comedy staple—overlapping dialogue. And in one year, he wrote and directed three hit films: *The Great McGinty* (1940), *Christmas in July* (1940), and *The Lady Eve* (1941). This strange, wonderful, greatly talented man, whose black and biting satire was almost the antithesis of Frank Capra's optimism, rounded out the evolution of the screwball comedy in the highest style and rejuvenated comedy in one fell swoop.

> 1) **A pretty girl is better than an ugly one.**
> 2) **A leg is better than an arm.**
> 3) **A bedroom is better than a living room.**
> 4) **An arrival is better than a departure.**
> 5) **A birth is better than a death.**
> 6) **A chase is better than a chat.**
> 7) **A dog is better than a landscape.**
> 8) **A kitten is better than a dog.**
> 9) **A baby is better than a kitten.**
> 10) **A kiss is better than a baby.**
> 11) **A pratfall is better than anything.**
> —**The Laws of the Box Office, according to Preston Sturges**

He was born in 1898 in Chicago to a wealthy family. His mother, Mary Dempsey, had always wanted to sing on the stage, and so Preston and his mother left for Paris, where they hooked up with the queen of all modern dance, Isadora Duncan. Sturges' seemingly fractured childhood was split between bohemian Paris, his education in France, Switzerland, and Germany, and the strict Chicago conventionality of his stockbroker stepfather, Solomon Sturges III.

The younger Sturges volunteered as a flyer in the army air corps during World War I, before and after which he worked for his mother's cosmetics company and, believe it or not, invented kiss-proof lipstick. By the age of twenty-five, he had married heiress Estelle Mudge, though she kicked him out four years later for his laziness. He bummed around New York as an inventor, devising a plate-glass carrier for trucks and a photo-engraving process. He tinkered with planes. While recovering from an appendix operation, he whipped off a little comedy called *Strictly Dishonorable*, which became the Broadway hit of 1929.

Universal Studios may have dropped him as screenwriter of their film version, but Sturges' time would come. In 1930, he was traveling across the country on a train when he met and fell in love with the heiress granddaughter of cereal king C.W. Post. They eloped, but divorced two years later. Inspired by his new, albeit temporary, patriarch, he wrote a screenplay about a tycoon called *The Power and the Glory*, with which he barged into the office of Hollywood mogul Jessie Lasky at Twentieth Century Fox. Lasky was sold, and Sturges' career was on a roll.

Through the 1930s, he wrote a string of successful screenplays. The action was anarchic (food fights were not uncommon). The dialogue was sparkling and often lethally edged. And the plots were fanciful, to say the least: in *Easy Living* (1937), secretary Jean Arthur's life is changed completely when a sable coat that a millionaire has thrown off a penthouse roof during a marital spat lands on her shoulders as she rides her bus to work.

That's Why the Lady Is a Vamp

When Sturges saw Barbara Stanwyck reading from his script for *Remember the Night* (1940), he approached the great star and gushed, "I'm going to write a great comedy for you!" Stanwyck dryly replied, "I never get great comedies," to which Preston pressed on, "Well, you're going to get one."

Henry Fonda is putty in Barbara Stanwyck's well-practiced hands in the funny, sexy The Lady Eve (1941).

By the next year, while killing time in Reno during his third divorce, Sturges had done a little rewriting on English playwright Monckton Hoffe's tale *Two Bad Hats*, about a snobby British lord who falls for a feisty American gal but won't marry a commoner, so she has to impersonate her own sister to get him. Sturges' version, *The Lady Eve*, pitted a priggish but impressionable American beer scion (Hopsie Pike, played by Henry Fonda) with an affinity for herpetology (a king snake named Emma) and a human watchdog of a chaperon (Mugsy) against the wiles of a card sharper (Colonel Harrington) and his daughter/accomplice (Jean Harrington/Lady Eve), only to have him fall for her. She, of course, fleeces him and in turn falls for him, before tumbling the two into a series of elaborate and comical twists.

For Stanwyck, this Cinderella, complete with cinders, let her be stronger, funnier, and perhaps sexier than she had ever been before. She wore the longest bob a star had ever sported (sixteen inches [41cm]) and turned heads in twenty-five different outfits. She steamed the screen in one of the sexiest scenes film has ever created: lounging

> *I have no success formula. If I have attained any, it's an act of God that I learned, as my Filipino chauffeur learned to drive an automobile. For five years he rode on seats near the bus driver and watched the driver. Then he went out and started driving.*
> —**Preston Sturges to columnist Hedda Hopper, on directing**

in an ocean-liner cabin and running her hands though Hopsie's hair—rendering him putty in the process. It was the role of a lifetime.

For her costar Henry Fonda, his first comedic role gave him a crash course in physical comedy. There is hardly a mishap that doesn't happen to Hopsie as he "falls" under Jean's sultry, savvy spell. He trips over her shapely gams twice, knocking over a few waiters in the process. He falls over a sofa, face-first into an appetizer tray. He pulls a block of boxes down on his head. He has roast beef and gravy dumped in his lap, gets soaked by hot coffee, sits in sloppy mud, is bonked by an apple, and even gets slobbered on by a horse—for which sugar lumps were plastered to the back of his head. Ironically, though he lived through as many as twenty-nine takes of some of these knockabout stunts without a scratch, during one of his last scenes—a love scene, no less—in which he was called to the phone, Fonda forgot that he was performing on a three-foot (91.4cm) platform and took a tumble, bruising himself, spraining his wrist, and gashing his knee. On the plus side, he got more kissing time (five hundred filmic feet [152m] of it) than he ever had before in his historical films *Young Mister Lincoln* (1939) or *The Grapes of Wrath* (1940), as well as fourteen costume changes of his own.

Fonda and Stanwyck weren't the only people with costume changes in this cinematic circus. Sturges wore weird hats on the set—his derby, flat straw hat, Swiss mountaineering hat, or double deerstalker—so that he would be easy to find. He constantly plied his cast and crew with coffee and seldom sat down except to play the piano during scene changes. His script was just about as wacky as he was, with less-than-lofty stage directions stuck in, such as, "She's a sweetie in a sweater," "He takes a gander at her gams,"

Eddie Bracken (right) is hoping that he's not the father in question as Betty Hutton and William Demarest watch him sweat in the raspberry blown at American morality, The Miracle of Morgan's Creek (1944).

"Unfortunately, as he says this, he looks like an idiot," or "He smiles like a gargoyle." He gave consummate conman Charles Coburn (as Colonel Harrington) such fatherly words as "Let us be crooked but never common" and "Women who cease to attract men often turn to reform as a second choice." Sturges even saddled his comedic regular Eric Blore (as Sir Alfred McGlennan Keith) with the inexplicable scene opener, "It was a white one with enormous teeth."

Sturges was stunned by Stanwyck's portrayal of Lady Eve, claiming that she'd anticipated his every comment and had a complete grasp of the character. Stanwyck shrugged, "The performer can't work miracles. What's on the paper is what's on the screen." Preston had made good on his promise and would continue to make a string of iconoclastic movies satirizing Hollywood in *Sullivan's Travels* (1941), marriage and greed in *The Palm Beach Story* (1942), Americana in *The Miracle of Morgan's Creek* (1944), and heroism in *Hail the Conquering Hero* (1944) before teaming up with producer and fellow aviator Howard Hughes and beginning his downward slide.

ABOVE: Joel McCrea gives Veronica Lake a ride just before he goes incognito in Sullivan's Travels (1941). RIGHT: Marisa Tomei and Michael Keaton keep the screwball spinning in The Paper (1994).

What a caper! What a romance! What a movie! *The Lady Eve* (1941) won an Oscar for Best Original Story and was voted best film of the year by the *New York Times*, beating out Frank Capra's *Meet John Doe*, John Huston's *The Maltese Falcon*, and Orson Welles' *Citizen Kane*. Never before had the screwball worlds of rich and poor, dishonest and upright, man (in this case, delightfully dumb) and woman (wickedly wise) collided so perfectly, so viciously, so erotically. And it was so cloaked and dizzy that there was nothing the Breen office could do about it.

NONSTOP ENTERTAINMENT

Now that you're president of Worldwide Pictures, it's your turn to screw up. In the interest of economy, you've decided to slap a series of romantic comedies into one enormous reel and call it Battle of the Sexes. Sure, the running time will be something like five days, but continuous showings have never been easier, and if your exhibitors threaten to leave your distribution, so what? It's not as though anyone else is standing in line to get your job. In fact, your new junior vice president is hovering nearby with helpful words of encouragement (though she does seem to be holding something sharp behind her back).

So, go ahead, make your megamovie. But remember, there has to be continuity. Each picture on the reel has to share a leading lady or leading man with the picture before and after it. For example, Sleepless in Seattle (1994)—Hanks and Ryan; When Harry Met Sally (1989)—Ryan and Crystal; Forget Paris (1995)—Crystal and Winger. The players you have to work with are: Cary Grant, Carole Lombard, Gary Cooper, Rosalind Russell, William Powell, Claudette Colbert, Melvyn Douglas, Myrna Loy, James Stewart, Ginger Rogers, Spencer Tracy, Irene Dunne, Katherine Hepburn, Fred MacMurray, Jean Arthur, Clark Gable, Don Ameche, Jean Harlow, Joel McCrea, and David Niven. Now go to work, you big mogul, you—before they scrape your name off the door!

A) Mr. Deeds Goes to Town *(1938)*

B) Take a Letter, Darling *(1942)*

C) Mr. Blandings Builds His Dream House *(1948)*

D) The Philadelphia Story *(1940)*

E) His Girl Friday *(1940)*

F) Midnight *(1939)*

G) Saratoga *(1937)*

H) Life with Father *(1947)*

I) Reckless *(1935)*

J) Bluebeard's Eighth Wife *(1938)*

K) Vivacious Lady (1938)

L) The Feminine Touch *(1941)*

M) The Ex-Mrs. Bradford *(1936)*

N) Once Upon a Honeymoon *(1942)*

O) The Thin Man *(1934)*

P) My Man Godfrey *(1936)*

Q) The Gilded Lady *(1935)*

R) She Married Her Boss *(1935)*

S) The Palm Beach Story *(1942)*

T) Too Many Husbands *(1940)*

U) Alice Adams *(1935)*

V) You Can't Take It with You *(1938)*

W) Holiday *(1938)*

X) Hands Across the Table *(1935)*

Y) Bachelor Mother *(1939)*

Z) Pat and Mike *(1952)*

AA) A Guy Named Joe *(1944)*

BB) Libeled Lady *(1936)*

CC) It Happened One Night *(1934)*

DD) The Primrose Path *(1940)*

Answers: D) Stewart and Hepburn, U) Hepburn and MacMurray, B) MacMurray and Russell, I) Russell and Powell, O) Powell and Loy, C) Loy and Grant, E) Grant and Russell, L) Russell and Ameche, F) Ameche and Colbert, JJ) Colbert and Cooper, A) Cooper and Arthur, M) Arthur and Powell, P) Powell and Lombard, X) Lombard and MacMurray, Q) MacMurray and Colbert, R) Colbert and Douglas, T) Douglas and Arthur, V) Arthur and Stewart, K) Stewart and Rogers, N) Rogers and Grant, W) Grant and Hepburn, Z) Hepburn and Tracy, AA) Tracy and Dunne, H) Dunne and Powell, BB) Powell and Harlow, G) Harlow and Gable, CC) Gable and Colbert, S) Colbert and McCrea, DD) McCrea and Rogers, Y) Rogers and Niven

Though the grand chemistry experiment of screwball comedy was largely taken off the front burner when WWII began, half a century later filmmakers are still trying to match the magic and mayhem of these classics. When Michael Keaton and Marisa Tomei rush to beat a newspaper deadline in *The Paper* (1994), they're tipping their hats to Cary Grant and Rosalind Russell in *His Girl Friday*. When Keaton and Geena Davis play speechwriters in love and combat in *Speechless* (1994), you know they've learned their craft from Spencer Tracy and Katherine Hepburn in *Adam's Rib* (1949). When Hugh Grant charmingly bumbles and stumbles in *Four Weddings and a Funeral*, he's only following in the footsteps that fellow clods like Gary Cooper and Jimmy Stewart.

Chapter Four

JUST NUTS

Though this be madness, yet there is method in it.

—William Shakespeare, *Hamlet*

Stella Stevens waits for Jerry Lewis to make a Jekyll and Hyde transformation into something a little suaver in The Nutty Professor (1963).

Kevin Kline have walked away from it with an Oscar if he hadn't been completely crazy?

Gonzo comedies are a little larger and more ludicrous than life, and we love them for it—if only because they make us seem more normal. It takes special kinds of people to play extreme farce: they can't be shy and stuffy, and they've got to do much more than pratfalls. Physical and facial expression and commitment are the names of this game. Certainly, the Marx Brothers and Abbott and Costello made their own kind of gonzo, but it took comic icon Jerry Lewis to give comedians permission not just to be childlike, but downright infantile and physically free!

Singing with his parents' act from the age of five, busting his stand-up comedy chops in the Borscht Belt of the Catskills in upstate New York, Jerry teamed up with crooner Dean Martin in Atlantic City, New Jersey, in 1946, and got very hot very quickly. Martin's silky suaveness gave Lewis license to be just the opposite: a complete geek with buckteeth, flapping arms, flopping feet, and a high-pitched, nasal,

Funny word, commitment. On the one hand, it can mean giving 110 percent of yourself to an undertaking with every fiber of your physical being, every ounce of your energy, every particle of your personality. On the other hand, it can mean being put away in a loony bin. Perhaps there's a connection. We have to admit that some of the movies that we've laughed at hardest and longest didn't make any sense at all.

Indeed, the strength of some movies is their strangeness. What would *Arsenic and Old Lace* (1944)—two nice old ladies poisoning people who come to visit them—be if it wasn't weird? Would Don Knotts have made such a splash if he hadn't taken the crazed physical plunge to become *The Incredible Mr. Limpet* (1964)? Would Pee-Wee Herman have risen so high before his fall if he hadn't been a mama's boy in *Pee-Wee's Big Adventure* (1985)? Would *A Fish Called Wanda* (1988) have spawned much attention if John Cleese, Michael Palin, and Jamie Lee Curtis had not been more than a tad demented? And would

ABOVE: Such sweet old ladies (Jean Adair, at left, and Josephine Hull)—it's too bad they like to poison nice old men. Cary Grant calls for help in Arsenic and Old Lace (1944). RIGHT: Jerry Lewis is a spaghetti Svengali in My Friend Irma Goes West (1950).

Dean Martin (left) explains to his partner why he is so lucky that he gets to carry both sets of clubs.

hysterical whine of a voice—the works. The duo hit it big with little parts in *My Friend Irma* (1949) and had spun out sixteen hit films of their own by 1956. When Martin quit, Lewis began studying film-making under the supervision of Frank Tashlin, director of some of Lewis' earliest solo film hits. By the late 1950s, Lewis was writing, directing, and producing his own wacky vehicles: *The Geisha Boy* (1958), *The Bellboy* (1960), *Cinderfella* (1960), *The Errand Boy* (1961), *The Patsy* (1964), and *The Disorderly Orderly* (1964) all bear the Lewis stamp, and *The Nutty Professor* (1963) may be his master-piece. Twenty-one hits of his own later, Lewis was not only a come-dy god in France (where they thought him the successor to Chaplin) but an inspiration to a generation of other geeks and goons to come stumbling after him.

"C'mon, Boys, We're Going over the Top!"

By the age of fourteen, Mel Brooks was already making money cracking jokes to guests around the pool of a Catskill Mountains resort. After serving in WWII, he hooked up with fellow funnyman Sid Caesar and became one of Caesar's head writers on the fifties television comedy hit *Your Show of Shows*, pulling in $5,000 a week.

When the show closed, so did a lion's share of Mel's career. He tried playwriting, but it seemed a comeback wasn't in the cards—until he teamed up with fellow *Your Show of Shows* alumnus Carl Reiner, with whom he recorded the now-famous 1960 comedy album *2,000 Years with Carl Reiner and Mel Brooks*. The two-thousand-year-old man was total Brooks, a wizened weisenheimer who had seen everything.

Looking brainy with the hit sixties comedy series *Get Smart* didn't hurt him, and neither did writing and narrating the Oscar-winning short *The Critic* (1964). Still, people always asked the causti-cally funny and irascible writer, "So, what are you working on?" For years, Brooks' sarcastic answer had been, *Springtime for Hitler: A Gay Romp with Adolf and Eva in Berchtesgaden*, a takeoff on Edward Everett Horton's play *Springtime for Henry*. Then, one day Brooks thought about it: cutting-edge comedians like Lenny Bruce had long joked about Hitler, but do a musical about him? It would be the biggest flop ever made.

And so, *The Producers* was born—a filmic jab at the Broadway that had spurned him. Its hero was a corpulent, seedy, charismatic impresario, Max Bialystock, who has been reduced to inveigling checks for his flops out of elderly patronesses through bizarre sexual favors. When Bialystock meets a meek and hysteria-prone accountant named Leo Bloom, who, while kindly burying a $2,000 discrepancy for him in his books, muses that a producer could make more mon-ey by raising really big capital for a flop than for a hit (if he over-sold shares in the show and pocketed most of the money). Lightning strikes, and Bialystock brazenly sets off, with Bloom in tow, to pro-duce the worst piece of drek in Broadway history.

The way Brooks pitched it to Oscar-winning producer Sidney Glazier must have been much funnier. Glazier practically fell out of his office chair laughing, and even without a script, he commit-ted himself to raise $600,000 for the project, an amount nearly equaled by Embassy Pictures distributor Joseph E. Levine, who con-tributed another $500,000. Neophyte director Brooks agreed to keep his fee small if he had the rights to the final cut. Next came casting for this carnival. Brooks knew just which actors he wanted.

Zero Mostel was a mountain of a man with almost as much tal-ent as he had flesh. He was one of the most consummately expres-sive comedians of this century. Yet his film output was very small. Why? He'd been screwed.

The son of a Brooklyn rabbi, Zero (as he was nicknamed as a kid) graduated from New York's City College with a degree in art, later moving to radio and then to a plum part in the Broadway show *Keep 'Em Laughing*. From there, he was picked to do Broadway comic legend Bert Lahr's dual role of Swami Rami/Cagliostro for the MGM musical *DuBarry Was a Lady* (1943). The door was shut when

I'll make a picture about making a picture. It'll be all nakedness and dirtiness and kissing and filth and nice. It'll be about a family in New York with four sons. All boys. But wait. They'll say four boys is no good. We got to get a girl. Make one of them a daughter with big bazooms. Then they'll worry about Dubuque. Bring in a farmer. With a daughter. Half naked. What's the name of the family? Gordon? Too Jewish. They'll change it to Whiteonwhite. Robert Whiteonwhite. Wait a minute. New York is too Jewish! Keep it in a tenement, but make it Akron, Ohio. A tenement in Akron, Ohio. Now you've got to have an orgy scene. What's the father, a pattern maker? Change him to a gypsy king. The king of the gypsies in a tenement in Akron, Ohio. Wait a minute. Make them all girls. Change the other three boys to gypsies. What do you think? The colored question is good and bad. Make one of the daughters a colored girl. With big bazooms. The Japanese market is opening up, right? So, the farmer's daughter is Japanese. With big bazooms.

—Mel Brooks in action, already dreaming of his next tasteful film before beginning shooting on The Producers *(1968), as told to* Variety's *Ronald Gold*

he was fired for making "leftist remarks" in public.

Mostel was briefly allowed to sneak back into Hollywood for a few supporting roles in the early 1950s, but Senator Joseph McCarthy put an end to that. Not only was Mostel blacklisted from Tinseltown, but he was banished from Broadway for almost a decade, so he turned to supporting himself by painting and performing abroad. When the door of American conservatism started creaking open again in the early sixties, Mostel made good by winning three Tony Awards for Best Actor for his dazzling, volcanic, comedic work in *Rhinoceros* (1961), *A Funny Thing Happened on the Way to Forum* (1962), and *Fiddler on the Roof* (1964). He was even welcomed back west as he reprised his crafty slave Sudulus in the fine 1966 film version of *A Funny Thing Hap-pened on the Way to the Forum.*

Brooks pounced like a panther to get the star for his first film. He gave Mostel the script that he had labored over; Mostel read it and gave a resounding no. "What's this?" he demanded. "A Jewish producer going to bed with old women on the brink of the grave? I can't play such a part, it's sick!" Brooks begged him to read it again, after which Mostel said, "I like it a little better, but the answer is still no. I just don't want to do it." In a last-ditch effort, Brooks used emotional blackmail in demanding that Mostel show the script to his wife, a friend of Brooks', and see what she thought. He charged, "You have to do that. This is very important. I've spent two years writing this thing, and I had you in mind all the time. I bought your paintings when nobody

ABOVE: Mel Brooks had been watching a tad too much Alfred Hitchcock when he made his famous spoof High Anxiety *(1977). BELOW: Zero Mostel (right) has a brainstorm that will make Gene Wilder either a millionaire or an inmate, in the wildly wacky* The Producers *(1968).*

else would, so you owe me this." A week later, Brooks got a call from Kate Mostel telling him that she loved it and would work on her obstinate husband. A week after that, Zero called, grumbling, "You son of a bitch. I'm gonna do it. My wife talked me into it."

For the nebbish Bloom, Brooks had someone much less established in mind, but just as perfect. The son of a Milwaukee manufacturer, Gene Wilder had studied acting at London's Old Vic and had trod the boards in America with Brooks' talented wife, Anne Bancroft, in a production of Bertolt Brecht's *Mother Courage*. Wilder and Brooks hit it off, and the young actor became a frequent houseguest at Brooks and Bancroft's summer home at Fire Island, New York. It was there that Mel had said to him, "I've got a great idea for a movie, and you're the only one I want for this part." Three years later, Wilder's star had risen a little, playing a nervous undertaker in *Bonnie and Clyde* (1967). He was in a Broadway production of Murray Schisgall's hit, *Luv*, when there was a knock at his dressing-room door. It was Brooks, who grinned and said, "You didn't think I forgot, did you?"

Nevertheless, with the demanding Mostel at the helm, Wilder had to audition for the great man, and he was petrified. He remembered walking into the office where Brooks, Glazier, and Mostel were waiting for this grave moment: "Zero gets up and walks toward me and I'm thinking, 'Oh God, why do I have to go through this again? I hate auditions, I hate them.' Zero reached out his hand as if to shake hands, and then put it around my waist and pulled me up to him and kissed me on the lips. He gave me a big kiss on the lips and all my fears dissolved."

Like Brooks, Mostel took Wilder under his wing, enabling him to become what Wilder later called "a neurotic bud that blossoms into a neurotic flower." He even repositioned Wilder's seat next to his own in the limelight at a May 1967 press conference, where the newcomer had been relegated to the periphery. On the set, Mostel allowed Wilder to shine by toning down his own riveting histrionics at key moments, but he didn't use the same kid gloves with Brooks during their eight-week shoot.

Fireworks were frequent between these two actors, but what a performance they produced. As the driven Bialystock (someone who would yell out through his grimy window at a white Rolls Royce pulling up across the street, "That's it, baby. If you've got it, flaunt it!"), Mostel is practically an irresistible force of nature. And how he can move.

His face!—the opening credits alone display it in all its glory through a freeze-frame succession of leers, sneers, coy looks, and

pleas for mercy as he does his gigolo gig with an investor he has dubbed "Hold me! Touch me!" (a very game, eighty-four-year-old Estelle Winwood). His body!—in a night scene beside the fountain at Lincoln Center, where Bloom makes up his mind to commit to criminality, Mostel's celebrating silhouette is more limber and expressive than any dancer's. As Zero had lamented, "They don't know what to do with me. Movie directors are used to shooting guys who don't know how to move or walk.

Zero (left) and Gene (right) enjoy hearing their playwright (Kenneth Mars) literally sing his Führer's praises in **The Producers.**

They use a lot of close-ups. They've just got to back off a little. My whole body does it, not just the eyes."

Despite the clashes, Brooks must have listened as he yelled. According to critic Charles Champlin, Mostel was "a definitive, septic study in low cunning and soaring chutzpa." There are so many memorable moments in this gag-packed film: Bloom's losing it in Bialystock's office—"I'm hysterical! I'm hysterical!"; after Bialystock has thrown water on him, "I'm wet and I'm hysterical!";

ABOVE: An indulgent Brooks (left) looks on as his cast frolics through the horror spoof *Young Frankenstein (1974)*. BELOW: Coming to a post-office wall near you: the criminal face of Virgil Starkweather (Woody Allen) in *Take the Money and Run (1968)*.

after Bialystock has slapped him in the face, "I'm wet, I'm hysterical and I'm in pain!" There's the duo's uncomfortable visit to the world's campiest (and best cross-dressed) director, Roger De Bris (played by respected director Christopher Hewitt). There's the panache of Bialystock's flagrant bribery of the *Times* critic on opening night (hoping to ensure a pan).

The supporting characters are no less brilliant. As Franz Liebkind, the nutty Nazi soldier–turned-playwright (though he still wears his helmet, even with white tie and tails), Kenneth Mars is so driven in his quest to clear Hitler's name that were it not for Mostel's and Wilder's performances, he would have stolen the show. No less can be said of Dick Shawn's comic turn as Lorenzo Saint Dubois (LSD), an over-the-hill flower child (watch for his Love Power musical audition), who actually plays Hitler as a hipster.

In *The Producers*, the boys sell shares to backers totaling twenty-five thousand percent of *Springtime for Hitler*, and as the curtain goes up on kicklines of singing storm troopers quipping such gems as "Don't be stupid, be a smarty, come and join the Nazi party"— well, you just have to see the slack-jawed faces of the audience to believe it. Brooks had joked, "What I want from this picture is another Academy Award. Or a car. A nice white car would be good, too." He got his wish. The Oscar for Best Script in 1968 went to the worst play Broadway ever produced. *The Producers* began Brooks' rise as one of America's premier comedy directors as well as a working

friendship with Wilder that would flower in two more 1974 comedies of legendary laughs, the western spoof *Blazing Saddles* and the horror spoof *Young Frankenstein*. As far as the white car goes, you'll have to ask Mel about it yourself.

future Schnook

Imagine a distant future where everyone looks terrific and is confident in the discovery that eating fatty foods and cigarette smoking are actually the best things you can

> What's this? I go in for an operation and wake up 2,000 payments behind in my rent.
> —Woody Allen, in *Sleeper (1973)*

do for your health. Picture a totalitarian state where Rod McKuen is revered as a classical influence on poetry, where recreational highs have been replaced by a metal orb passed around to party guests, and where all the men are impotent (except those of Italian

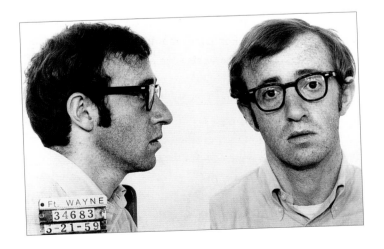

And it looks like fun. Woody Allen's dubbed Japanese thriller, What's Up, Tiger Lily? (1966).

The inspiration for the futuristic *Sleeper* came to Allen when he was filming the hilarious, high-tech "sperm sequence" (in which he plays a commando sperm) for *Everything You Always Wanted to Know About Sex*. Though he first pitched the idea to United Artists as a four-hour film in which the first half would be a contemporary New York comedy ending with Woody getting frozen, only to be thawed after intermission for the futuristic second half, the final vision was only future. This time, with a $2 million budget that expanded to $3.1 million, Allen shot *Sleeper* in the 100° F (37.8°C) heat of

extraction), so couples have to go into an Orgasmitron to have sex. Now visualize a mousy, intellectual, kvetching, neurosis-laden, sex-obsessed New Yorker waking up in this world after being cryogenically frozen for two hundred years after a botched ulcer operation...and being sent (because of his anonymity) to infiltrate a top-secret government project counting only on the assistance of a screwy, beautiful pseudo-artist named Luna.

Got the picture? If so, your mind is on its way to being as twisted as Woody Allen's when he thought up the script for his ninth and zaniest movie ever, *Sleeper* (1973). But Allen had quite a head start. In high school, he was already selling jokes to Earl Wilson's newspaper column and a New York public relations firm. After flunking out of New York University in 1953, he joined the NBC writer's program, wrote for *The Garry Moore Show*, and was eventually drafted into the same extraordinary pool of writing talent on Sid Caesar's *Your Show of Shows* that produced Mel Brooks.

Yet it was doing his own material as a stand-up comedian in the Catskills in the 1960s and developing his neurotic everyman performing persona that really gave Allen his career boost. After three popular comedy albums, he got his shot at the big time rewriting the script for *What's New, Pussycat?* (1964), about a playboy's wacky attempts to give up infidelity. The movie made so much money—$17 million—that Allen was given another shot at a project of his choice.

What kind of mind would take a Japanese spy thriller and radically redub it into English so that the plot revolves around detective Phil Moscowitz and his search for the stolen recipe for the world's greatest egg salad? That would be the mind that made *What's Up, Tiger Lily?* (1966), a film so successful that in 1969 Allen was given a $1.6 million budget to write, direct, and star in his own movie, *Take the Money and Run*. He took the money and ran through the subsequent hits *Bananas* (1971), *Everything You Always Wanted to Know About Sex But Were Afraid to Ask* (1972), and the adaptation of his hit Broadway play *Play It Again, Sam* (1972). An American comic institution had been born.

Monterey, California; among the futuristic-looking homes of Boulder, Colorado; and on the old David O. Selznick set for *Gone With the Wind* (1939). During the 101-day shoot, he would indulge his taste for science fiction, his love of Dixieland jazz, and his reverence for silent comedians. There are bits scattered throughout the 22nd-century sojourn of Miles Monroe, a Greenwich Village health food store proprietor, that lovingly steal from virtually all the great silent clowns. The newly revived Miles not only looks like a bespectacled Harry Langdon as he eats blue baby food, but during a visit from local storm troopers he playfully misbehaves in a motorized wheelchair just the way you would expect Charlie Chaplin to in *Modern Times*. Miles trapped inside an inflatable suit that is speedily deflating across the surface of a lake (which took five days to shoot because the tow rope kept breaking) pays homage to Buster Keaton's *The Navigator*, as does the bungling assistance he gets from leading-lady liability Diane Keaton, reminiscent of so many "helpful" Buster Keaton heroines. And Miles dangling from computer tape from the window of an office building is certainly a bit that Harold Lloyd would have appreciated.

Talking clowns get respect, too. The bit where a nervous Miles bites Luna's fingernails instead of his own (as they

> He is, as he has always been, a unique comic personality, as consistent and fully realized as Chaplin's tramp or Keaton's sad-eyed bumbler or W.C. Fields' well-oiled curmudgeon. Allen is a kind of high IQ, modern, urban everyman, sprung full-grown and edgy from an analyst's couch, electric-haired, and anxious-eyed behind the horn rims, obsessed with girls, insecure and neurotic, ceaselessly verbal, with wall-to-wall fantasies largely furnished by the movies.
> —*Los Angeles Times* critic Charles Champlin on Woody Allen, in a December 12, 1973, article

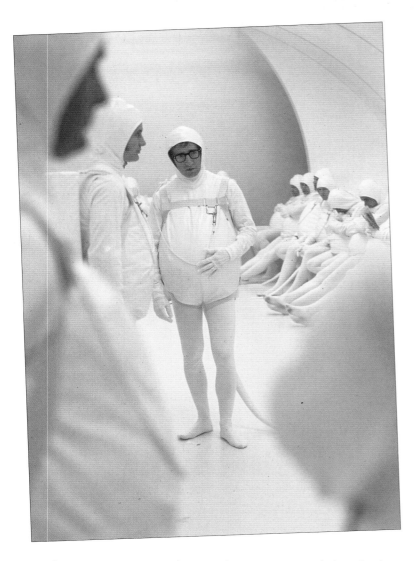

Woody takes another potshot at the then-bellicose New York head of the United Federation of Teachers, when he has scientists explain that World War III transpired when "a man by the name of Albert Shanker got hold of a nuclear warhead." And Allen even gets a jab in at his ex-wife, Harlene, when Miles relives the trauma of telling his parents that he is divorcing his wife, Arlene: "She thinks I'm a pervert because I drank our waterbed."

Some verbal gems are strung together seemingly spontaneously. In an info-session with scientists, Miles goes through an array of twentieth-century artifacts and artfully explains their significance. On Stalin: a communist with an unpleasant mustache he wasn't too crazy about. Bela Lugosi: former mayor of New York City. Charles DeGaulle: a famous French chef. F. Scott Fitzgerald: a romantic writer popular with college girls, English majors, and nymphomaniacs. Chiang-kai Shek: not crazy about him, either. Billy Graham: knew God personally and used to double-date with the Deity. Norman Mailer: a great American writer who donated his ego to the Harvard Medical School. Richard Nixon: the Secret Service counted the silverware after he left the White House.

impersonate surgeons who are going to reconstruct their society's assassinated dictator by cloning his nose) is pure Bob Hope, whom Allen has always credited as a big influence on his work. "Hope was always a superschnook," said Allen. "He looks less like a schnook than I do, though....Both of us have exactly the same wellspring of humor. There are certain moments in his old movies when I think he's the best thing I have ever seen. It's everything I can do not to imitate him." And Hope would agree that seeing Allen exploit the physical side of his trademark verbal self is a rare treat. What could be more classic than raiding a field of mutant vegetables—"I'd hate to see what they use for fertilizer"—only to slip on a ten-foot (3m) banana peel?

Allen made his film's soundtrack vintage, too. "As we're setting the film in the future," he stated, "I wanted to get away from all those Moog synthesizers, and we ended up with a ragtime score"—one that Allen, of course, wrote himself and played clarinet for, accompanied by no less than the Preservation Hall Jazz Band and the New Orleans Funeral and Ragtime Orchestra. Allen had learned the clarinet at age sixteen by listening to George Lewis records, so it was only fitting that when he was through with his recording session with the Preservation Hall band, ancient trombonist Jim Robinson approached him and said, "Did anyone ever tell you that you sound like my friend George Lewis?"

All this shtick and music doesn't mean that *Sleeper* isn't just as hip as any other Woody Allen movie. On the topic of God, Miles confesses to Luna (as only he could), "I think there's an intelligence governing the universe, except certain portions of New Jersey."

ABOVE: Miles experiences premature inflation. RIGHT: Miles goes incognito as an android butler and gets a little overattached to the recreational drug of the future, the Orb.

And Howard Cosell: viewing him was punishment for citizens who had committed crimes.

Improvisation was more than in the air, as Allen changed his mind constantly on the set. In a bedroom scene with actress Christina Forbes, the director first donned an aviator costume and brought in a tornado-creating wind fan. Then he canned the fan and had Forbes eating from a huge bowl of cottage cheese and oranges. Next, he changed into a wetsuit. Finally, he scrapped the whole thing.

By the time Allen had finished filming, he had an embarrassment of film riches—200,000 feet (60,960m), 240 reels, thirty-five hours. He would trim his little film down to a two-and-a-half-hour rough cut and, eventually, an eighty-eight-minute final cut. As Allen's editor, Ralph

CALLING ALL NEUROTICS

Let's see what kind of Woody connoisseur you are. In his more than twenty-six films, this American comedy maestro has manifested his self-obsession in a riotous variety of personae. Your job is to match up the oddball everyman to the appropriate movie.

Neurosis

1) This loser may cook his meat with the cellophane still on, but he's man enough to become the leader of a tropical country in turmoil.

2) This demented nephew of 007 has plans (as the evil Doctor Noah) to rid the world of all men over a certain height—his own.

3) This failed Russian revolutionary's gratitude, when the beautiful Sonia nobly agrees to sleep with him before he faces a firing squad, amounts to "Nice idea. I'll bring the soy sauce."

4) This cradle-robbing television writer's short list of reasons to live includes Groucho Marx, Willie Mays, the second movement of Mozart's "Jupiter" symphony, Louis Armstrong playing "Potato Head Blues," Swedish films, Flaubert's A Sentimental Education, Marlon Brando, Frank Sinatra, Cézanne's still lifes, crabs from Sam Woo's restaurant, and Tracey's face.

5) This klutzy comic's idea of fun is drawing out an escaped lobster from behind the refrigerator with a dish of drawn butter.

6) This dismally dedicated theatrical agent can only untie himself from slinky mob-widow Tina Vitale by writhing rhythmically and erotically to the floor with her.

7) This German hardware clerk sets out to capture a serial killer, armed by his landlady with pepper to throw in his eyes, and notes, "Very good. I'll ward him off with a seasoning."

8) This sweaty-palmed felon regrets having carved his gun out of soap.

9) This love-starved bachelor manages to be rebuffed even when his married friends set him up with a notorious nymphomaniac.

10) This jealous documentarian keeps a close female colleague from interviewing a famous television producer by saying, "When you see Lester later, be careful. Because if this guy tells you he wants to exchange ideas, what he wants to exchange is fluids."

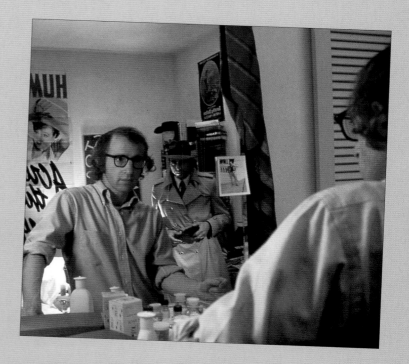

11) This hysteria-prone comedy director calls the pigeons that fly into his apartment "rats with wings."

12) This human chameleon takes on the appearance and personality of whomever he's with, be it Calvin Coolidge, Jack Dempsey, or the pope.

13) This Wall Street financier/inventor's gadgets include a device for putting bones into fish.

14) This middle-aged lawyer's deceased mother is appearing to him in the sky just to convince him to get over his shiksa and marry a nice Jewish girl.

15) This hypochondriacal television producer is convinced that "there's a tumor in my head the size of a basketball."

16) This brave biologist lures a giant runaway breast into a gigantic bra.

17) This meek Manhattanite may suspect foul play in the apartment next door, but he still tells his sleuthing wife, "There's nothing wrong with you that a little Prozac and a polo mallet wouldn't cure."

18) This puzzled English professor has fallen for an impressionable twenty-year-old student with a list of older conquests as long as his arm.

Nebbish

A) *Sheldon in "Oedipus Wrecks" from* New York Stories *(1989)*

B) *Gabe Roth from* Husbands and Wives *(1992)*

C) *Max Kleinman from* Shadows and Fog *(1992)*

D) *Jimmy Bond from* Casino Royale *(1966)*

E) *Boris Grusenko from* Love and Death *(1975)*

F) *Ike Davis from* Manhattan *(1979)*

G) *Alvy Singer from* Annie Hall *(1977)*

H) *Danny Rose from* Broadway Danny Rose *(1984)*

I) *Cliff Stern from* Crimes and Misdemeanors *(1989)*

J) *Larry Lipton from* Manhattan Murder Mystery *(1993)*

K) *Mickey Sachs from* Hannah and Her Sisters *(1986)*

L) *Virgil Starkweather from* Take the Money and Run *(1969)*

M) *Andrew from* A Midsummer Night's Sex Comedy *(1982)*

N) *Leonard Zelig from* Zelig *(1983)*

O) *Fielding Mellish from* Bananas *(1971)*

P) *Allan Felix from* Play It Again, Sam *(1972)*

Q) *Victor Shakapopulis from* Everything You Always Wanted to Know About Sex But Were Afraid to Ask *(1972)*

R) *Sandy Bates from* Stardust Memories *(1980)*

Answers: 1=O, 2=D, 3=E, 4=K, 5=G, 6=H, 7=C, 8=L, 9=P, 10=I, 11=R, 12=N, 13=M, 14=A, 15=F, 16=Q, 17=J, 18=B

Rosenblum quipped, "Digging a grave at a cemetery would be funnier to watch than two guys cutting a comedy." During the radical surgical process, scads of scenes bit the dust. Among the best may have been a romantic dining sequence where an aroused Miles eats his napkin and one of Luna's candlesticks. What was perhaps the highest concept in the whole film took a similar powder. Scientists looking in on Miles' unconscious through a "dream visualizer" found our hero dressed as a white pawn on a giant chess board (shot on a salt flat in California's Mojave desert). When a black knight who has just maced and impaled another pawn turns to him, Miles nervously chirrups, "Hey fellas...it's only a game. We'll all be together later in the box," but to no avail. Though he manages to cop a feel with the queen before bolting from the board, his dream segues into a packed concert hall, and transforms him into a violinist whose bow goes flaccid.

Allen readily admits the frustrations of his experimental process: "I'll watch the dailies and I'll think none of those walks looks funny and I'll reshoot them and when I go to edit the film and I cut those walks in, the two worst ones in the dailies will get the biggest laughs. There are so many factors you're bucking. That's why film comedies are so hard." There's little doubt that we're lucky he's taken *Sleeper* and his other films so seriously. Still, one can't help but wonder what a megareel of Allen outtakes and lost scenes would look like.

Virtuosity

If screwball comedy depicts the war between the sexes, what do you call it when that war is waged within one hapless, human body? Androgyball comedy? Nah! Just call it very chancy, very loony, and very, very funny. Girls have tried to pass for guys, and vice versa, in countless comedies, but the first to implode it into one showstopping yet believable performance was Steve Martin (with ample help from Lily Tomlin) in Carl Reiner's fourth collaboration with the master funnyman, *All of Me* (1984).

Ed Davis' (penned under the name Edwina) book about soul transmigration, *Me, Two,* was originally bought by King's Road Entertainment for less than $100,000 as a vehicle for Katherine Hepburn and Lee Marvin. Kate would play a ninety-nine-year-old dowager who is transmigrated into the body of a derelict named Al (Marvin), and all sorts of funny things would happen when the profane yet ladylike Al visited the dowager's family. The film didn't get made. Thank heaven for small favors.

Producer Stephen Friedman bought it and gave it to television newsman–turned-screenwriter Phil Alden Robinson to tinker with.

Not bad having an angel on your shoulder, says daffy director Carl Reiner.

After he transformed the character of the dowager into Edwina Cutwater, a very rich and chronically bedridden spinster, he gave her the idea to transmigrate her soul to the beautiful young body of her stableman's daughter, Terry, through the aid of a swami. The transfer (via a brass ceremonial bowl) at the moment of her death goofs when her lawyer, Roger Cobb, happens to be walking underneath her window

> I suspect I'm the first to play both sexes simultaneously, with either side of my body.
> —Steve Martin

as the just-soul-filled bowl comes flying down and conks him on the head, admitting the newly deceased Edwina in—and giving her control over the left half of his body. That would be wild enough, but now the struggling, uncoordinated Roger has to deal with his philandering boss, a stuffy fiancé, the gold-digging Terry, and a myriad of other obstacles as he tries to shed himself of the soul that is inhabiting (and moving) part of his body. Worse yet, he begins to care about Edwina's happiness.

A concept this bizarre attracted the likes of Emmy-winning director Carl Reiner, a third writing alumnus of *Your Show of Shows*, who had not only acted in such classic comedies as *It's a Mad, Mad, Mad, Mad World* (1963), *The Russians Are Coming! The Russians Are Coming!* (1966), and *Where's Poppa?* (1969), but managed to cowrite and direct television's *The Dick Van Dyke Show*,

> The gags are funny and they're extended by Martin with a physical virtuosity worthy of Buster Keaton. His walk, for example, is a masterpiece of reluctant androgyny: his left leg moves out with macho snap, followed by the mincing lilt of his right leg.
> —Jack Kroll, *Newsweek* magazine, on *All of Me*

produce (so to speak) son Rob Reiner, and collaborate with comedian Steve Martin on his three phenomenally successful films *The Jerk* (1979), *Dead Men Don't Wear Plaid* (1982), and *The Man with Two Brains* (1983).

Surely, that wild and crazy guy Steve would be willing to play half a man and half a woman. Didn't he get rich dressing up as King Tut and regularly wearing an arrow through his head? He'd love it. Or maybe not. When Reiner called Martin to pitch this outlandish script, the comedian demurred: "Eh, Robin Williams is really right for it. It sounds like something *he* could do." Luckily, Reiner made Martin read it, after which he changed his tune to "Forget Robin Williams." Martin was in.

In finding the perfect match to play and provide the voice for this free spirit trapped in a rich spinster's—and then a hapless lawyer's—body, Reiner hired character chameleon Lily Tomlin. Tomlin, who had grown up in working-class Detroit, worshiping comediennes such as Lucille Ball, Bea Lillie, Jean Carroll, and Imogen Coca, had graduated from television's *The Garry Moore Show* and *Laugh-In* to her own Tony award winning one-woman Broadway show, *Appearing Nightly*, and such hit films as Robert Altman's *Nashville* (1975), *The Late Show* (1977), and *Nine to Five* (1980). Like Martin, her roots were in stand-up comedy, featuring such extreme characters as Crystal the hang-gliding paraplegic.

LEFT: Mirror, mirror on the wall, who's in the most trouble of them all? That would be Steve Tomlin (or is that Lily Martin?) in All of Me (1984). OPPOSITE: A tender moment for Roger and Edwina at the end of a virtuoso performance.

AND NOW FOR SOMEONE COMPLETELY DIFFERENT

It may have been the weirdest, but All of Me *was hardly the only comedy where one gender/age/race has had to switch with its counterpart. Ever since Cinderella passed for a princess and Dr. Jekyll flipped to Mr. Hyde, Hollywood has put actors through changes that a shapeshifter would be proud of. See if you can find the films and players that go with the following phenomena.*

1) Can blind, legless vet (in reality, street hustler) Billy Ray Valentine really make money walking in commodities-broker Louis Winthrope III's wingtips?

2) This starving cabaret singer finally gets her big Parisian break when she plays a man playing a woman.

3) Will actor Michael Dorsey find success, happiness, and even love while masquerading as hospital administrator Dorothy Michaels? Tune into Midwest General to find out.

4) Three's a crowd when Rita Boyle's spirit trades places with an old man's during her wedding to Peter Hoskins.

5) Adolescence was bad enough! Now Annabel Andrews has to deal with midlife crisis because she has switched bodies with her mom, Ellen.

6) Dr. Jack Hammond no longer scoffs at ancient Navajo medicine, now that it has switched his body with Chris', his teenage son.

7) Twelve-year-old Josh Baskin got just what he asked for and is a little nostalgic for his "lost youth."

8) When racist L.A. cop Jack Mooney gets a new lease on life thanks to newly deceased black lawyer Napoleon Stone, his redneck behavior changes color.

9) This groundbreaking cross-dresser looked good in mohair and made some of the most popular cult films ever.

10) Wide receiver Robert Muldoon may have had the best hands in the NFL, but Roberta Muldoon takes better care of them.

11) If Daniel Hillard ever wants to spend any time with his kids, he'll have to brush up his housekeeping skills and wear a lot of makeup.

12) This lawyer's career could become dog-doo if he doesn't stop turning into a canine.

13) He's just a sweet transvestite from Transsexual, Transylvania.

14) When Jerry and Joe witness Chicago's Valentine's Day massacre, Daphne and Josephine hide out with an all-girl band in Florida.

15) This flock of Florida retirees aren't exactly getting older, thanks to a little extraterrestrial help.

16) Two dress like women and one used to be a man, but they're the most entertaining troopers the outback has ever seen.

17) Take three of Hollywood's butchest leading men and let them camp around America's heartland, as Noxema, Vida, and Chi-Chi, and—voila!

18) Mark Watson is about discover what a little melanin change means to a guy at Harvard Law School.

ANSWERS: 1) Eddie Murphy and Dan Aykroyd in Trading Places (1983), **2)** Julie Andrews in Victor Victoria (1982), **3)** Dustin Hoffman in Tootsie (1982), **4)** Meg Ryan and Alec Baldwin in Prelude to a Kiss (1992), **5)** Jodie Foster and Barbara Harris in Freaky Friday (1976), **6)** Dudley Moore and Kirk Cameron in Like Father, Like Son (1987), **7)** Tom Hanks in Big (1988), **8)** Bob Hoskins and Denzel Washington in Heart Condition (1990), **9)** Ed Wood in Glen or Glenda? (1953), **10)** John Lithgow in The World According to Garp (1982), **11)** Robin Williams in Mrs. Doubtfire (1993), **12)** Dean Jones in The Shaggy D.A. (1976), **13)** Tim Curry in The Rocky Horror Picture Show (1975), **14)** Jack Lemmon and Tony Curtis in Some Like It Hot (1959), **15)** Wilford Brimley, Jessica Tandy, Hume Cronyn, and Don Ameche in Cocoon (1985), **16)** Terence Stamp, Guy Pearce, and Hugo Weaving in The Adventures of Priscilla, Queen of the Desert (1994), **17)** Wesley Snipes, Patrick Swayze, and John Leguizamo in To Wong Foo, Thanks for Everything! Julie Newmar (1995), **18)** C. Thomas Howell in Soul Man (1986)

Tomlin was ready for the challenge of Edwina—a woman who would be onscreen all of fifteen minutes but whose voice would run through Martin's head (and ours) for two hours.

Just how would you set about creating a character eccentric enough to dip her pills in caviar and wash them down with Dom Perignon, and pluck embroidered tissues from a jeweled tissue dispenser (both bits devised by Tomlin)? The actress began by studying a wealthy woman she had met at a health spa. As Tomlin noted, "I got fixed on her to learn the preoccupations of profoundly rich people. Did you know Barbara Hutton could spend two or three hours at a stretch looking at her jewels?" Once into character, Tomlin videotaped a list of little, feminine mannerisms for Martin to study and perfect, and she arrived on the set whether her physical presence was needed or not. As Martin remembers, "There are scenes where we hear only her voice. Those scenes are usually recorded later, but she wanted to be there to feed me her lines, to make sure the timing was just right."

That timing often took twelve to fifteen takes, but still the duo had fun together. At first, Roger doesn't believe he's hearing Edwina's voice in his head ("I must be picking up General Hospital in my fillings"), but seeing is believing when Edwina's reflection greets him in the bathroom mirror as he brushes his teeth. In preparation for this magical scene, Tomlin bounced around in her nightgown, singing "Wonderful, Wonderful, Copenhagen" to accompany Martin as he jogged around the set in his boxer shorts.

This isn't to say that no one went out of his way for her. In one scene where she had to be desolate, Martin remembers valiantly coaching her: "I was depressing her. I was saying things about her dog." And in another scene in which Roger/Edwina finds that he/she is the only one at Edwina's memorial service, Tomlin found some unexpected sympathy. It seems the "Funeral Services for Edwina Cutwater" sign posted outside the Methodist church where the film was shooting in the Hancock Park area of Los Angeles attracted mourners. "Six people came in off the street, claiming to know the deceased," Tomlin recalled. "It was very touching."

Speaking of touching, the scene in which the one-sided, one-handed Roger, in order to do his business in the men's room, has to vociferously persuade the horrified Edwina to provide manual, if not exactly coordinated, assistance in easing his bladder, has to rank with the funniest scenes ever filmed. And the scene in which Edwina has to argue a case in court, posing as her better half when his half falls asleep, is so side-splitting that it shouldn't be legal. As Martin said of the scene, "In other words, I'm a man pretending to be a woman pretending to be a man."

With the help of Reiner, Tomlin, and supporting characters, including yet another former Your Show of Shows writer, Selma Diamond (whom Reiner claimed "could read the Yellow Pages and put you on the floor laughing"), as Roger's gruff secretary, and veteran Second City improviser Richard Libertini as the plumbing-fixated guru ("It's the first character I've ever played who has no lines," Libertini said. "All I do is repeat whatever anyone says to me...and hum a lot"), Martin carries off the androgynous performance of the

Forget the Pepsi generation; they're living in the Stone Age. The heavenly gift of this Coke bottle (dropped from a passing plane) is going to cause a lot of mischief before it's recycled in The Gods Must Be Crazy *(1982).*

decade. The sweetly celebratory dance in the final frames couldn't be more fitting. And though he may have joked, "I can't wait to read my reviews, the one that says, 'loved her, hated him,'" critics were so awestruck with both that he became a comedy superstar.

Sweet Insanity

From South Africa, the land of apartheid, came one of the wackiest, most life-affirming cult comedies ever made, and its charismatic star was a four-foot (1.2m)-tall bushman named N!xau from the Kalahari desert (the ! represents a tongue click, of which there are twenty-one in his language). Before filming began, he had only seen two whites and one vehicle in his entire life. So much for expensive acting lessons and an agent.

Veteran director Jamie Uys' The Gods Must Be Crazy (1982) is a must, if unique is what you seek. Picture a happy family of hardy bushmen in Africa's southern desert living the simple life, with no concept of work, no property ownership, no crime—just harmonious hunting (narcotic-tipped arrows drug their prey, to which they apologize before killing), gathering (they drink precious water from tree roots and dew from leaves), and survival. Into this parched paradise, a Coke bottle drops from a passing private plane. The bushmen find that their mysterious gift can be used for grinding grain, crushing roots, smoothing snakeskin, stretching thongs, making patterns on cloth, and even making music. Suddenly, it's a hot commodity in a place where no commodities have existed before. Jealousy erupts. Fights break out. A boy is bonked on the head with it. One of the bushmen, Xixo (N!xau), takes matters into his own hands. When he tries to throw the bottle back up to the gods, it falls back and hits his daughter on the head. There's nothing left but for him to throw the evil object off the edge of the world.

That's just where the adventure begins. There is a whole collection of nut cases for Xixo to run into beyond the desert. There's a big-city reporter (Sandra Prinsloo) who has chucked it all to teach in rural Botswana. There's the manly microbiologist (Marius Weyers) who has been sent—in a Land Rover called the Antichrist that can't be turned off and has no brakes—to fetch her but in whose presence he becomes more accident-prone than Chevy Chase. There's his crusty, cursing, three-wived mechanic (Michael Thys); an oily tour guide (Nic De Jager) competing for the reporter's attentions; and even a bumbling but bloody terrorist (Louw Verwey) and his band, whose path they all stumble into.

Worlds collide as Xixo makes his sojourn into civilization. And as unlikely allies join forces to rescue one another from potential disasters, the heart is warmed as much as the funny bone is tickled. Loony behavior abounds in this little gem, but without the wink-wink nudge-nudge that often sneaks into mainstream movies. Sure, Smokey the Rhino charges a campsite to stamp out a camp-fire (rhinos do that). Yes, the Land Rover's winch hoists it up a tree while the microbiologist tries to untangle his half-naked passenger from a thorn bush (a Land Rover will do that if left unattended). Of course, a bottle-stealing baboon gets a stern lecture from the heroic Xixo (as we know, bushmen respect animals). Sound wild? Making the movie was even wilder.

The role of Xixo was cast after Uys had traveled seventeen thousand miles (27,358km) of desert (with an interpreter, as more than one thousand dialects of the bushman language exist) to interview hundreds of potential actors. N!xau became the only movie star who ever opted to sleep on his hotel room floor during filming, took breaks to report back to his family about the escalators and elevators that the gods had made, and put a stop to production when his stomach and buttocks doubled their size (bushmen are capable of living on one enormous meal for a week; the three-meal-a-day schedule of the filmmakers was a gift to him and a curse to them).

Shooting on the Etosha pan brought real-life dangers that most comedy directors don't usually figure into their budgets. In one scene where a poison-spitting Egyptian cobra was filmed with utmost care by the crew (the cameraman wore a patch on his non-viewfinder eye, only to have the snake spit into the lens), N!xau walked over, grabbed the serpent, and dashed its brains out against a rock, as most of the crew fainted. And a shot in which the microbiolo-

gist inspects a tranquilized elephant became distinctly untranquil when the pachyderm awoke ahead of schedule and charged the crew (you can see the wobble in the camera). When Uys filmed Weyers and Prinsloo struggling across the Limpopo river, he heard that crocodiles were eating swimmers, so he stationed riflemen up-and downstream to shoot into the water every five minutes, telling the curious cast that it was just the sound of local hunters. And while thick clouds obscured the view the first day that it came time for N!xau to toss that Coke bottle from the cliff top called God's Window, the second day's clarity petrified the bushman—after all, he had never been higher than the low desert in his life. Uys had to wrestle with his crew near the precipice to show his star how safe it was.

Crowd scenes were no cinch, either. In a triumphant sequence in which an entire village greets their new teacher in song, bored kids poking around with sticks enraged eighty thousand killer bees, which swarmed the entire valley and forced cast, crew, and inhabitants to clear out for two full days. However, the honey of a reception that *The Gods Must Be Crazy* received in Europe, Japan, South America, and the United States ($52 million in the United States alone) must have taken the sting out of any bee sting. After three years of filming (Uys took hiatuses as he ran out of money) and one and a half years of editing and sound recording, Uys had the kind of good-hearted hit on his hands that gave him what any director hopes for—a sequel, *The Gods Must Be Crazy II* (1989).

The Ghost with the Most

Funny? Would you call a ghoul with a mouthful of rotting teeth, a face full of fungus, a head of dog hair, a slobbering, gravelly voice, a huckster's penchant for deception and uncontrolled lechery, and a taste for insects funny? Well, let's not be hasty. Crazy people can be funny. Elwood P. Dowd (Jimmy Stewart) and his 6-foot (1.8m)-tall

Such a nice couple—too bad they're dead.
Constance Bennett and Cary Grant spook Roland
Young in Topper *(1937).*

wanted to be Vincent Price (Price himself narrated it). He was even wackier with the short *Frankenweenie* (1982), about a boy who brings his mutt back from the grave. His first oddball feature, directing another fine comedian, Pee-Wee Herman, in *Pee-Wee's Big Adventure* (1985), was a psycho-smash. Then, Warner Brothers offered him $1 million to direct the sequel to *Gremlins* (1984). He had something else in mind.

Why not do "a comic version of *The Exorcist* from the dead people's point of view"? A movie that would have the romantic leads killed off in the first ten minutes? A film that would wait to introduce the title character halfway through? A story that would make the dead people much more attractive than the living cast? Why not pump $14 million of vintage and state-of-the-art special effects into it—including split screen, blue screen, black screen, creature and mechanical effects, rod-and-cable-controlled puppets, stop-motion photography, replacement animation, rotoscope, 1/87th scale models and miniatures of whole towns, motion control, front lite/back lite mattes, rear-screen projection, forced perspective, and two-way

ABOVE: Lovable lunatic Elwood P. Dowd (Jimmy Stewart) poses for a publicity still with a six-foot (1.8m) Pookah rabbit that's better left to our imagination in Harvey (1950). RIGHT: Beetlejuice talks to some folks with worse problems than his as he waits to see his caseworker in the netherworld social work office.

Pookah rabbit sweetly showed us so in *Harvey* (1950). Super-neurotic, multiphobic Bob Wiley (the incomparable slob, Bill Murray) was lovable even though he drove his psychiatrist to distraction in the priceless *What About Bob?* (1991). Tragicomic Robin Williams was delightfully delusional as *The Fisher King* (1991). A field-tripping quartet of psychotics (Peter Boyle, Christopher Lloyd, Michael Keaton, and Stephen Furst) who were separated from their shrink on the way to a Yankees game managed to medicate us with a lot of laughs in *The Dream Team* (1988).

Dead people can be funny, too. Cary Grant and Constance Bennett were witty spirits in *Topper* (1937). Constance Cummings was pretty comedic in Noël Coward's ghostly farce *Blithe Spirit* (1945). Bill Cosby was an awfully cute *Ghost Dad* (1990). So wouldn't it stand to reason that a crazy ghost would be twice as funny?

Former Disney animator Tim Burton had already been crazy like a fox with his cartoon, *Vincent* (1982), about a little boy who

At some point you show up on the set and just go fuckin' nuts.
—**Michael Keaton, cameo star of *Beetlejuice* (1988)**

mirrors? Why not sneak in kitschy filmic references to other weird films, like *The Cabinet of Doctor Caligari* (1919), *Topper* (1937), *Halloween* (1978), *Dune* (1984), *The Fly* (1984), *A Nightmare on Elm Street* (1984), and *Little Shop of Horrors* (1986).

What bizarre story could merit all this attention? *Beetlejuice* follows a charming yuppie couple, the Maitlands (Alec Baldwin and Geena Davis), who charmingly drown in a car crash on the way back from a trip to the hardware store. Condemned to "haunt" their picturesque Victorian house in Connecticut for 125 years, they finally have the leisure time they've been craving.

Or do they? When the dreadful Deetz family (Jeffrey Jones, Catherine O'Hara, and Winona Ryder) from artsy Soho, New York, move in and begin to remodel their domicile tastelessly, the Maitlands try to spook them out—in a nice way. They even possess the Deetzes' dinner-party guests (who include Dick Cavett) in an involuntary calypso dance to Harry Belafonte's "Day-O," complete with face-sucking shrimp cocktail.

Unfortunately, the Deetzes find the ghosts trendy and even envision a theme park at the homestead. The Maitlands are forced to consult their *Handbook for the Recently Deceased* and descend to the creepy, hysterical, bureaucratic depths of the underworld. There, beyond a waiting room that includes special-effects wizard

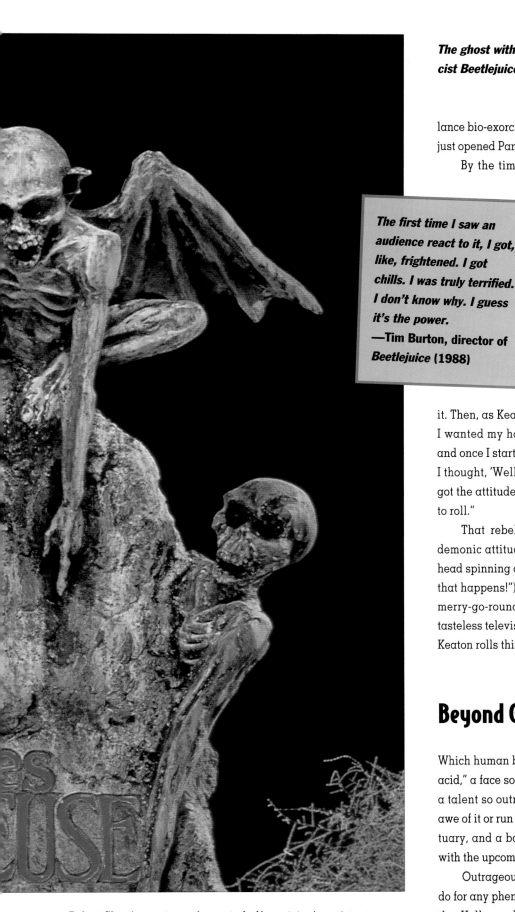

lance bio-exorcist" named Beetlejuice (Michael Keaton). They have just opened Pandora's laugh box.

By the time Beetlejuice arrives, the movie is weirder than weird. When Keaton was first offered the part, the title character had been even weirder. Keaton would have turned it down had Burton not made him an offer he couldn't refuse—the freedom to write some of his own shtick. Keaton went home and began his journey beyond bizarre. Working from the outside in was the ticket for a spirit who largely created his own reality. First came the gravelly, slobbering, redneck voice. Then came an engagingly ghoulish face, and the dissipated paunch to go with it. Then, as Keaton remembers, "I started thinking about my hair. I wanted my hair to stand out like I was wired and plugged in, and once I started getting that, I actually made myself laugh. And I thought, 'Well, this is a good sign. This is kind of funny.' Then I got the attitude, and once I got the basic attitude, it really started to roll."

> The first time I saw an audience react to it, I got, like, frightened. I got chills. I was truly terrified. I don't know why. I guess it's the power.
> —Tim Burton, director of Beetlejuice (1988)

That rebellious, lascivious, lightning-tongued, demented, demonic attitude will roll you into the aisles. From Beetlejuice's head spinning around on his body like a top ("Ugh!!! I hate it when that happens!") to his body turning into a giant snake or a human merry-go-round with octopus-hammer hands to making his own tasteless television ads to (slobber! slobber!) wedding a teen bride, Keaton rolls this performance and flick right into the hall of fame.

Beyond Gonzo

Which human being has the hyper-expressive body of "Astaire on acid," a face so mobile that it seems to crawl off his head at times, a talent so outrageous that moviegoers either stand in complete awe of it or run screaming to *Masterpiece Theater* for tasteful sanctuary, and a bank account that now grows $20 million by a film with the upcoming Cableman?

Outrageous stories have sprung up about Jim Carrey, as they do for any phenomenon. Did he, as an unknown, really stand up in the Hollywood Hills telling himself he was famous until he believed his own mantra? Did he really write himself a check for $10 million to be cashed on Thanksgiving, 1995? We can only guess.

We do know that he was born near Toronto, Canada, and grew up in hard times (his dad lost his job, and Jim dropped out of high school at age thirteen to help support the family). He was

Robert Short's creations of a cut-in-half magician's assistant, a scuba-diver half swallowed by a shark, a still-smoking smoker in bed, a camper in her sleeping bag with a rattler, a shrunken-headed great white hunter, and a smashed hit-and-run victim, their crusty caseworker (Sylvia Sydney) tries to help them. And with the assistance of the Deetzes' morbid daughter, Lydia (Ryder), the Maitlands lower themselves in desperation to enlisting the services of "a free-

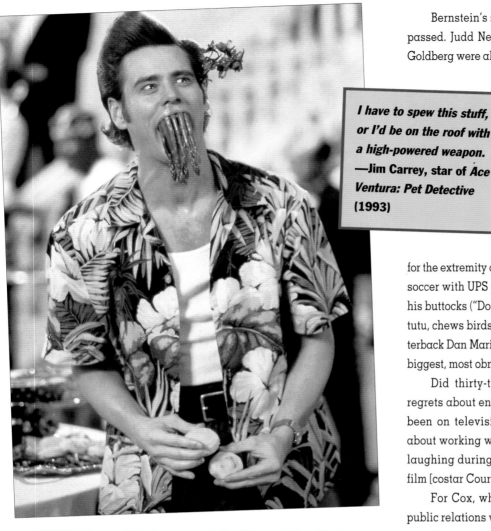

Bernstein's script was originally offered to Rick Moranis, who passed. Judd Nelson, Alan Rickman, Steven Weber, and Whoopi Goldberg were also considered, but Morgan Creek Productions finally courted Carrey, and did it for two years. He hated the script. When they agreed to pay him $450,000, allowed him to rewrite it, and gave him the option to walk away from it if he still disliked it, Carrey took the bait. "I saw the character had to be rock 'n' roll," said Carrey. "He had to be the 007 of pet detectives. I wanted to be unstoppably ridiculous, and they let me go wild."

> I have to spew this stuff, or I'd be on the roof with a high-powered weapon.
> —Jim Carrey, star of *Ace Ventura: Pet Detective* (1993)

They did, indeed. There are no words for the extremity of Carrey's performance as a macho geek who plays soccer with UPS parcels, catches bullets in his teeth, talks through his buttocks ("Do you have a breath mint?"), runs football plays in a tutu, chews birdseed, makes exploding-toilet jokes, befriends quarterback Dan Marino, and, after unknowingly kissing a man, has "the biggest, most obnoxious homophobic reaction ever recorded."

Did thirty-three-year-old director Tom Shadyac have any regrets about encouraging his star to be even bigger than he had been on television? Shadyac admits, "The most difficult thing about working with Jim was trying to keep the cast and crew from laughing during takes. We had to send Jim off the set in order to film [costar Courtney Cox's] closeup lines."

For Cox, who played the role of love interest and Dolphins public relations woman, one of those closeups came during an intimate love scene back at Ace's love nest. It was just Carrey, Cox, and about fifty animals, including parrots, skunks, squirrels, dogs, monkeys, and penguins. In fact, Carrey and Cox's Olympian lovemaking generated a little too much animal lust. "All the animals had to be chained to their positions," recalls Cox, "but the squirrel would get loose and jump on the penguin, the penguin would bite the cockatoo, and soon all hell would break loose and I'd find myself under the blanket with a macaw."

Carrey is so compulsively inventive that he even studies his own

> We knew from the first day of shooting that we were way off the planet Earth. We would either make or destroy our careers. But Jim and I were in agreement that, if we were going to make a stink bomb, let's make a unique stink bomb.
> —Tom Shadyac, director of *Ace Ventura: Pet Detective*

face when he's depressed to add it to his arsenal of expressions. "I know there are acting teachers out there saying 'I didn't tell him to do that,'" says Carrey, but millions are glad he did. Though Carrey was originally offered a cool million to do *Ace Ventura: When Nature Calls* (1995), the original was such a hit that, three days after it opened, his asking price went up to $5 million. Carrey 's gleeful reaction to the sequel? "It's ten times worse. It's really, really sick. It's my ticket to the gates of hell."

ABOVE: The perfect dinner guest, Jim Carrey, in Ace Ventura: When Nature Calls (1995). OPPOSITE: Hey, who's that dapper-lookin' guy? Fred Astaire on acid? No—just Jim Carrey in The Mask (1994).

influenced by Jerry Lewis, Dick Van Dyke, and Charlie Chaplin; started entertaining in Toronto comedy clubs; became the king of impressions at L.A.'s famous Comedy Store (Sammy Davis, Jr., and Henry Fonda were headliners); and opened on the road for major acts like Rodney Dangerfield. He later ditched impressions at the Comedy Store to work on his improvisational comedy, and after a few small roles in movies such as *Peggy Sue Got Married* (1986) and a short-lived television series called *The Duck Factory*, he hit it big as the white comedian for four years on a more successful TV venture called *In Living Color*.

His big breakthrough feature, *Ace Ventura: Pet Detective* (1993), was long in coming. Writer Jack Bernstein, while watching an installment of David Letterman's "Stupid Pet Tricks," had dreamed up the ludicrous idea of a deranged but dedicated pet dick on the trail of an abducted bottle-nosed dolphin named Snowflake (mascot for the Miami Dolphins). He recalls, "There was a dog that could go into a convenience store; he could buy a pack of smokes and get change. And I thought to myself, what would the owner do if he lost his dog? What would he tell the police?"

Chapter Five

IS NOTHING SACRED?

Satire is a sort of glass, wherein beholders generally discover everybody's face but their own.

—Jonathan Swift, author of *Gulliver's Travels*

PEARLS BEFORE SWINE

No one zinged them out with less affectation or more outrageous hilarity than Fields.
Here are just a few of the swipes he took at just about everything. Here's W.C. on...

BEVERAGES	*"I never drink water. Fish fuck in it."*
FOOD	*"Somebody left the cork out of my lunch."*
DRINKING	*"I got Mark Hellinger so drunk last night that it took three bellboys to put me to bed."*
LOVE	*"I was in love with a beautiful blonde once and she drove me to drink: 'tis the one thing I'm indebted to her for."*
MORNING	*"I must have a drink of breakfast."*
DISCIPLINE	*"I exercise self-control, I never drink anything stronger than gin before breakfast."*
CHARACTER	*"Anyone who hates small dogs and children can't be all bad."*
POLITICS	*"I never vote for anyone. I always vote against."*
MAE WEST	*"A plumber's idea of Cleopatra."*
SEX	*"They say that drinking interferes with your sex life. I figure it's the other way around."*
GLAMOUR	*"She's all done up like a well-kept grave."*
HIS NOSE	*"Its red swollenness came from bruising it on a cocktail glass in my extreme youth."*
WOMEN	*"Women are like elephants. I like to look at them, but I wouldn't want to own one."*
BEING TOLD A HONEY-MOON SUITE WAS RESERVED FOR MEN WITH BRIDES	*"That's all right. I'll pick one up in town."*
SHOOTING BIRDS IN HIS YARD	*"I'll go on shooting the bastards until they learn to shit green."*
A 3-FOOT (0.9M) KING SNAKE CRAWLING ACROSS HIS SHOULDER	*"It cannot be. It does not happen. This of course, is a damnable allusion, a mere figment of the gin-inspired cerebellum. I shall, I will, be brave."*

The great one made a class exit. On Christmas Day, 1946, after having fallen into a coma, he suddenly awoke, looked at the two people standing by his bed (his secretary, Magda Michael, and a nurse), put his index finger to his lips for quiet, winked conspiratorially, and passed on to the great vaudeville circuit in the sky.

This Is the Way the World Ends...Not with a Bang but a Snigger

Stanley Kubrick's whole career had been fast-tracked. At seventeen, he was a staff photographer for *Look* magazine. By the age of twenty-four, he had written, directed, and shot his first feature, *Fear and Desire* (1953). His stark antiwar film *Paths of Glory* (1958) had (with the help of Kirk Douglas) launched him into the Hollywood firmament by giving him control of the heroic epic *Spartacus* (1960). He had followed up with a dark adaptation of Vladimir Nabokov's immortal, immoral *Lolita* (1962), and now, at thirty-five, the boy wonder wanted to do a serious film on nuclear warfare...at least, at first he did.

Kubrick claims to have perused sixty to seventy tomes on nuclear weapons during this time. He subscribed to such bedside reading as *Bulletin of the Atomic Scientists*, *Missiles and Rockets*, and *War Peace Report*. He even interviewed atomic experts such as Herman Kahn and Thomas C. Schielling. It was only when Alastair Buchan, the director of the Institute for Strategic Studies, gave him Peter George's tense 1958 novel *Red Alert* that he committed himself to a project. The book outlined the ensuing chaos when a hawkish General Quinten, who is suffering from a terminal disease, launches a nuclear attack on the U.S.S.R., necessitating the U.S. president to sacrifice Atlantic City, New Jersey, as an offer of peace. Kubrick was particularly chilled by the book's line "If the system was safe for 99.99 percent of the days in a year, given average luck, it would fail in thirty years."

Buying the rights for a mere $3,000, Kubrick set to work adapting *Red Alert*, with the help of George and author Terry Southern. The more serious they tried to make the story, the more absurd it became. Finally, they gave in and let the absurdity have sway. Quinten became General Jack D. Ripper, a raging, cigar-chomping, branch-water-drinking psychotic with an obsession about fluoridating the purity of his "precious bodily fluids," who gives a group of bombers the go code to attack the U.S.S.R. from his office at Burpleson Air Force Base.

When milquetoast President Muffley and the alerted White House order the base stormed, Ripper tells his troops that it's a disguised communist attack. Only an overly polite British group captain named Lionel Mandrake has a snowball's chance in hell to find Ripper's secret code, which will recall the bombers—that is, if an overzealous Colonel "Bat" Guano will let him. Meanwhile, back at the war room, chaos is breaking out. Much to the outrage of clownishly commie-hating General Buck Turgidson, the sneaky Soviet ambassador de Sadesky has informed Muffley that, should any bombs get through, a doomsday device will enshroud the entire planet in a nuclear cloud for a hundred years. Frantic

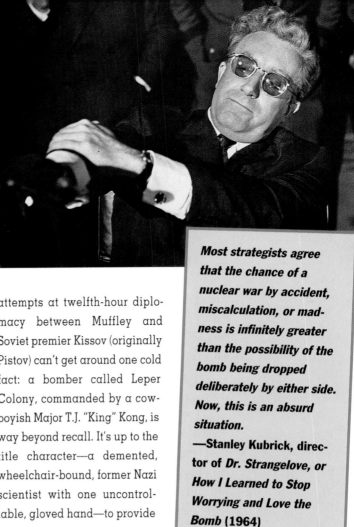

attempts at twelfth-hour diplomacy between Muffley and Soviet premier Kissov (originally Pistov) can't get around one cold fact: a bomber called Leper Colony, commanded by a cowboyish Major T.J. "King" Kong, is way beyond recall. It's up to the title character—a demented, wheelchair-bound, former Nazi scientist with one uncontrollable, gloved hand—to provide a final solution.

Sound startling enough? Kubrick's starkly realistic-looking, straight-played, black-and-white "nightmare comedy" (in his words) is an indisputable masterpiece of satire and the pioneer in making fun of American leadership's out-of-control war machine. As historian Lewis Mumford said, it was the "first break in the catatonic Cold War trance that has held our country for so long in its rigid grip."

Dr. Strangelove (1964) may have ruffled the feathers of a few hawks, but what film wouldn't, with two refueling bombers seeming to mate in midair to the tune of "Try a Little Tenderness" or flying to bring on Armageddon to "When Johnnie Comes Marching Home Again"? For a generation just going counterculture, the film became a milestone, and its edge owed as much to its acting as to its script.

George C. Scott was never more grandly gonzo than as the infantile, macho Buck Turgidson (who learns of the impending World War III while he is offscreen on the toilet). Sterling Hayden is the steeliest of psychos as General Ripper. Keenan Wynn (W.C. Fields' pal, and Ed's son) is the ultimate in that contradictory concept of military intelligence, as the Coke machine–shooting Colonel "Bat" Guano. Still, the main attraction can only be Peter Sellers. The

ABOVE: You can't keep a good arm down. Peter Sellers as the involuntarily "sieg heiling" Dr. Strangelove (1964). LEFT: Sellers (right) as U.S. President Milford Muffley, in détente with Soviet ambassador de Sadesky (Peter Bull) in the Pentagon War Room.

comedic genius had just come off a three-character chameleon stint in Kubrick's *Lolita* and was originally slated to bump up to four roles for *Dr. Strangelove*: Mandrake, Muffley, Strangelove, and Kong. However, the star was worried about being seen as doing an Alec Guinness (the master character actor had played eight aristocrats in *Kind Hearts and Coronets*, 1949). Sellers' problems were solved when, during the filming of his wheelchair-bound Strangelove sequences, he broke his ankle. Veteran cowpoke Slim Pickens subbed wonderfully as Kong ("Hell, boys, I guess it's toe-to-toe with the Ruskies").

Even down to three parts, Sellers was a movie marvel, but not a cheap one. When asked if he was getting "three actors for the price of one," Kubrick corrected, "You mean three actors for the price of six." Sellers was worth it. Although his first take on the president was a limp-wristed junkie, Sellers' very American bureaucrat is cunningly underplayed; here, he improvised much of his chatty phone call with the irate Soviet premier ("Well, how do you think I feel, Dimitri?"). As Colonel Mandrake, he is the personification of ineffectual English good sportsmanship, and totally endearing; his difficulty in aiding Ripper in the slaughter of incoming soldiers because the string is gone from "his gamy leg" is another stellar Sellers embellishment.

As Strangelove, Sellers is probably the creepiest that comedy ever gets (and, contrary to popular opinion, the portrayal was based more on physicist Edward Teller than on diplomat Henry Kissinger). That high-pitched, Teutonic voice (Sellers claimed that it was a German accent superimposed on that of the photographer Weegee's) and those demented digits of his right hand—replicating the real neurological disorder known as alien hand syndrome: twitching, grasping, raising in an involuntary Nazi salute, and even attempting to choke its owner—were also Sellers' idea. Kubrick thankfully did pull in the reins at a gloved masturbation scene.

Perhaps the most surprising thing about this film is that the original ending, which was worked on for nearly a fortnight, was scrapped. Mack Sennett would have been pleased. Designer Ken Adams' black, polished (the sixty actors in the scene were allowed to wear shoes only during actual takes) Pentagon War Room set was originally the site for the biggest pie fight in movie history. At least two thousand pies were ordered every day, and the cast got so much practice plastering one another that they were all outlawed from Sheperton Studio's commissary. After JFK's assassination in Dallas, Kubrick sensibly nixed Scott's line "They've cut down my president in his prime with a pie!" After a preview or two, the entire lighthearted sequence was axed. Its dark replacement has to "go down" as one of the most riveting

> *Everything that happened in the picture happened in a hospital somewhere at some time.*
> —Paddy Chayevsky, on his script for *The Hospital* (1972)

and, yes, Freudian endings a movie has ever had. And yes, shortly after the film was made, the Soviets did create a doomsday nuclear device. Isn't it nice when life imitates art?

Giving Them a Taste of Their Own Medicine

He may have been the best television and film writer America ever produced. He was certainly the angriest. Out of the ten film scripts that Paddy Chayevsky put on the screen in his tragically short career, almost a third of them won Academy Awards for writing. The Oscar-winning *Marty* (1955), based on an original teleplay, showed the desperate and self-perpetuating loneliness that many single people face in date-crazed America. *The Goddess* (1958) virtually shattered the glamour myth of stardom with Kim Stanley's tortured performance as a Marilyn-esque movie queen. *The Americanization of Emily* (1964) took the military down a satiric peg with a story of a naval officer who finds that he is to be the first casualty of the Normandy invasion. The Oscar-winning *Network* (1976) would take a comic but hellacious swipe at television and include a mad newscaster prophet (Peter Finch) whose words "I'm mad as hell, and I'm not going to take it anymore" would speak for a whole generation of angry Americans.

Dull bachelor Marty (Ernest Borgnine) and his mother (Esther Minciotti) have it out over a cup of tea before one of Marty's few-and-far-between dates.

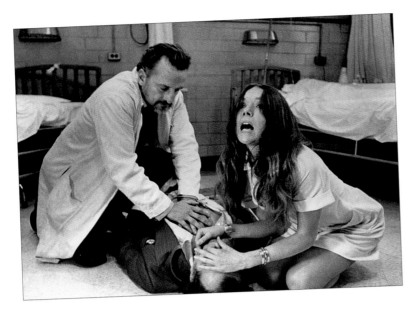

In the early seventies, the pacing, fuming, bearlike Chayevsky was notorious for speaking his mind in New York's Writer's Guild meetings. There was nothing that he didn't have a caustic, informed, blackly comic, unadulterated opinion on. The raw way he expressed it was often too much for some of the guild's more delicate members. As writer Jerome Lawrence remembered, "Paddy would take on anyone and anything."

He wanted to take on the medical establishment. His wife, Susan, was suffering from a mysterious and painful neurologic disorder that medical personnel were writing off as a woman's hysterical symptoms. One night, Paddy was walking the streets of New York with his friend Herb Gardner when he asked the fellow writer (of the excellent comedy *A Thousand Clowns*, 1966) if he knew "a good way to kill nurses." Chayevsky was soon pitching United Artists honcho David Picker a script idea about "a fuck-up in a hospital." As off-putting as the proposal was, the success of films such as *Butch Cassidy and the Sundance Kid* (1969) had made offbeat a good thing, and Picker accepted. Chayevsky had a minor stipulation, however: he wanted total control of the picture. To ensure it, he drafted lawyer and poker buddy Howard Gottfried to work as his producer. (Chayevsky once gushed, "He has no interest in whether you like him or not, which is one of the reasons I like him so much.")

The writer's research was, as he put it, "everything short of medical school." He read medical journals "by the truckload." He frequented New York's many hospitals, including one in the Bronx with an emergency room that he likened to "something out of a World War II movie." He read malpractice suits and interviewed dozens of hospital staff members, who were only too glad to share their horror stories because they, too, were mad as hell about medical bureaucracy. What he wrote was one of the most darkly funny movies of the fertile seventies, with what could be considered the acting performance of the decade.

The Hospital begins unsettlingly. Las Vegas show music blares as Chayevsky's own New York accent glibly narrates the horrible events that start the story, all in front of the close-up of a corpse of an old man who occupied a bed in Room 106 in the Holly Pavilion of New York's Manhattan Medical Center. Through a med-

ical mixup, his moderate emphysema has been fatally misdiagnosed as a heart attack.

With the man's sudden departure, the local studly intern, a Dr. Schaffer (coincidentally, the man responsible for the mistake) has used the empty bed for a boff with a hematology nurse during his night shift (a graphic scene reduced to a freeze-frame to avoid an X rating). The only other person in the two-bed room is a comatose old man who has mistakenly had one of his kidneys removed and the other kidney damaged since his arrival. After the tryst, Schaffer is snoozing solo when someone fills out the chart by his bed for a sedative injection and a glucose intravenous, which the night nurse mindlessly carries out. The problem is, the doc is diabetic and is soon stone dead.

Into the crisis ambles Dr. Herbert Bock, a grizzled, bearlike, former medical whiz kid and current fifty-something chief of medicine. He's newly separated, a raging alcoholic, estranged from his hippie son, impotent, and suicidally depressed, but he's one hell of a doctor and teacher with one hell of a temper and tongue. His diatribes are funny and bellicose enough to make you bust a gut—for instance, his final scream in a dressing down of his nursing chief: "Where do you train your nurses, Mrs. Christie—Dachau?"

As suspicious deaths of hospital staff start to multiply, and protests from the local citizenry, whom the hospital is evicting to make way for a drug rehab center, threaten a community takeover, Bock must rouse himself to meet the mounting chaos and incompetence. To make matters worse, amid the complaining nurses, greedy doctors, and frenzied patients strolls Barbara Drummond, the cool, calm, collected, extremely sexy twenty-five-year-old ex–acid head (and ex-nurse) daughter of the other patient in Room 106. She may be the answer to Bock's buried passion for living—or the force that finishes him off.

As far as Chayevsky was concerned, there was only one actor in America capable of playing the part of Bock. *The New Yorker* had dubbed George C. Scott "the king of the bums," and rightly so. He was the most dynamic actor of his generation...and a total mess. As famous for his wranglings with writers, his on-and-off-set brawls (his nose was broken five times), and his drunken absences as for his bravura acting, Scott wasn't merely qualified to play Bock—he was the genuine article. Scott wanted $300,000 (steep for the 1970s); United Artists wanted Walter Matthau or Burt Lancaster. Chayevsky held out for his star. Scott got his deal plus costar and director approval. Other roles went to a pool of veteran New York theater talent, including Nancy Marchand (as Mrs. Christie), Frances Sternhagen ("I know you doctors are the ministering angels and I'm just the bitch from the accounting department, but I have a job to do, too"), Richard Dysart (as a greedy medical entrepreneur), and sterling ensemble work by Stockard Channing, Katherine Helmond, Jacqueline Brooks, and Christopher Guest.

As the doctor who misguidedly operates on one of his own nurses, Bernard Hughes had just been on Broadway in *Abelard and Heloise*, "in which I castrated my daughter's lover, so I guess

Paddy was impressed with my surgical skill," he said. That daughter was none other than Diana Rigg, an extraordinary English actress whose black-leather-clad spy, Mrs. Emma Peal, on television's *The Avengers* had prompted London's *Tattler* magazine to claim that she "could probably read Proust, understand it, and knee a villain in the crotch at the same time." She was the Barbara Drummond who could quiet Bock's storm (Scott had vetoed the political Jane Fonda, as well as the studio's choices of Ali MacGraw and Candice Bergen). Rigg, however, turned down the offer, and only after Hughes set her straight about the opportunity that she was passing up did she reconsider.

What a cast! But no director? Just before the project went before the lenses, director Michael Ritchie (who had done *Downhill Racer*, 1969) was axed by Scott because they had disagreed on the physical condition of an operating room on the vacant floor of Metropolitan Hospital, which Mayor John Lindsay had rented to the film. Arthur Hiller, who had directed *The Americanization of Emily* and had originally priced himself out of this job, was called back with an offer for even less money than originally offered and one hour in which to make up his mind. He jumped at it.

More hurdles lay ahead. Scott, who had missed the first day of shooting and drunkenly watched television through the second and third, was going through his second horrendous divorce from the electric actress Colleen Dewhurst. He had officially snubbed the Oscars that April; when he won for his performance in *Patton* (1970), his son Campbell (now a rising actor) had to wake him up, for he had gone to sleep early that night. Scott went outside his upstate New York home, gave the waiting reporters a few words, and then went to memorize a three-page confessional to a hospital psychiatrist—his first shot of the picture. The next day, he knocked it off in one take.

Scott missed more days on *The Hospital* set, but once he was threatened with dismissal, he buckled down. It is amazing that for this funny, frenzied film, which gives Bock so many mammoth, wrathfully eloquent speeches (and which United Artists originally lobbied to cut), Scott agreed to rehearse for only one scene. In it, Bock unburdens his seared soul to Drummond, attempts suicide, and then

ravishes her when she intercedes. This six-page, three-minute-and-thirty-two-second behemoth of a scene was wrapped up in an excessive three takes.

At one point late in filming, Chayevsky felt Scott's Bock might be a tad too edgy for a popular comedy and, girding his own loins, approached the star in his dressing room (with producer Gottfried as backup). Scott, who had had a bear of a day, was leaning over to untie his shoes as Paddy nervously rattled off his adjustments. When Scott stood up, he stabbed the writer with his finger and screamed, "You do the fucking writing!" and pounded his own chest, adding, "And I'll do the acting!" Gottfried remembers that "he pounded himself so hard at the 'I'll do the acting,' I was sure that he had put his hand through his chest."

The producer and writer skedaddled, and maybe it's good they did. As doggedly true as he was to Patton, Scott was no less convincing, compelling (and this time, funny) as Bock. *The Hospital*

OPPOSITE: Another day, another donor. Things are running amuck as usual in The Hospital (1972). RIGHT: He's mad as hell and he's not going to take it anymore. A messianic Peter Finch in Paddy Chayevsky's Network (1976).

Sneak attacks of satire prove that laughter (at someone else's expense) is still the best revenge. Before Robert Townsend gave Hollywood a black eye with *The Hollywood Shuffle* (1987), the brothers Coen finked on the studio system with *Barton Fink* (1991), or Robert Altman made his play with *The Player* (1992), Blake Edwards had a certain ax to grind to perfection with a film called *S.O.B.* (1981)—Standard Operational Bullshit (though certain studio executives might well give the initials another meaning).

> How sharper than a serpent's tooth it is to have a thankless child.
> —William Shakespeare, *King Lear*

ABOVE: Which one is Roger Ebert? Jimmy Woodard (left) and Robert Townsend skewer the movie biz in The Hollywood Shuffle (1987). BELOW: All he's asking this family-picture star to do is expose her breasts in a sex film. Richard Mulligan pleads with Julie Andrews in S.O.B. (1981).

earned Chayevsky his third Oscar. The film came in under budget and under schedule, and inspired hard-edged satire for another generation. And thanks to you-know-who, there was so little footage to futz with that editor Eric Albertson had the rough cut ready one day after the shooting ended.

What else would you grind if Jack Warner had demanded a happy ending for your indictment of alcoholism, *The Days of Wine and Roses* (1962)? How would you feel if your *Darling Lili* (1969) was savaged for being wildly over budget? Would you take it personally if studio chief James Aubrey had done an edit-room evisceration on your western, *Wild Rovers* (1971), and relieved you of final surgical privileges for *The Carey Treatment* (1972)? In 1973, Edwards, whose comedy credits also included *Breakfast at Tiffany's* (1961), *The Great Race* (1964), and the celebrated Peter Sellers vehicles *The Pink Panther* (1963) and *A Shot in the Dark* (1964), decided to

Fear and Loathing in Paradise

Filmmakers taking Tinseltown to task is nothing new, as in: *Show People* (1928), about a former czarist general working as a Hollywood extra; *What Price Hollywood?* (1932), about an alcoholic director; and Bing Crosby's crooning vehicle *Going Hollywood* (1933). These films did more early scolding than scalding of the Dream Machine. On the other hand, Billy Wilder's completely unpleasant *Sunset Boulevard* (1950) made Hollywood a monstrous, murderous place. Since then, disgruntled writers in Babylon, be they Clifford Odets (*The Big Knife*), Nathanael West (*The Day of the Locust*), or F. Scott Fitzgerald (*The Last Tycoon*) have turned their bile to dialogue.

> I wrote the script ten years ago. It was turned down by everybody. Finally a man named David Picker, with Lorimar, did it. Then, he made a deal with Paramount to distribute it. When I heard that, I screamed. I said, "But I wrote it about Paramount!"
> —Blake Edwards, on his no-holds-barred Hollywood satire, *S.O.B.* (1981)

BITING THE BURG THAT FEEDS THEM

Ah, Sodom-by-the-Sea. Ya gotta love this town...at least while the cameras are rolling. Off camera, it's a different story. Bernardo Bertolucci may have dubbed Hollywood "the big nipple" in his Academy Award acceptance speech for The Last Emperor *(1987), but for many more directors, actors, and (especially) writers, this palm-lined paradise has been a ringside seat for the decline of Western civilization. Here is some of the best spoken abuse they've dished out over the past sixty years.*

"There's nothing wrong with Hollywood that six first-class funerals wouldn't cure."
　　　　　—anonymous, c. 1930

"Hollywood is a world with the personality of a paper cup."
　　　　　—Raymond Chandler, writer

"Hollywood is the only town where you can wake up in the morning and listen to the birds coughing in the trees."
　　　　　—Joe Frisco, comedian

"A cultural boneyard."
　　　　　—Marlon Brando, actor

"Strip the phony tinsel off Hollywood and you'll find the real tinsel underneath."
　　　　　—Oscar Levant, pianist

"Everybody kisses everybody else in this crummy business all the time....If people making a movie didn't keep kissing, they'd be at each other's throats."
　　　　　—Ava Gardner, actress

"Our town worships success, the bitch goddess whose smile hides a taste for blood."
　　　　　—Hedda Hopper, gossip columnist

"They've great respect for the dead in Hollywood, but none for the living."
　　　　　—Errol Flynn, actor

"The motion picture business is still the only one in which decisions are made by people without any experience in their field."
　　　　　—Blake Edwards, director

"They shoot too many pictures and not enough actors."
　　　　　—Walter Winchell, journalist

"Hollywood's all right. It's the pictures that are bad."
　　　　　—Orson Welles, director

"It's a great place to live—if you're an orange."
　　　　　—Fred Allen, comedian

"Of all the Christ-bitten places and businesses of the two hemispheres, this one is the last curly kink on the pig's tail."
　　　　　—Stephen Vincent Benét, writer

"The most beautiful slave quarters in the world."
　　　　　—Moss Hart, playwright

"It's impossible to tell where the DTs end and Hollywood begins."
　　　　　—W.C. Fields, comedian

"A warm Siberia."
　　　　　—anonymous

"Never in my life have I seen so many unhappy men making a hundred thousand dollars a year."
　　　　　—Nicholas Schneck, former head of MGM

"The only asylum run by the inmates."
　　　　　—Grover Jones, script doctor and Hollywood wag

"This is the only place I've ever heard of where the citizens practice stabbing themselves in the back in their spare time just by way of gymnasium work-outs."
　　　　　—Nunnally Johnson, writer

"I went out there for a thousand a week, and I worked Monday and I got fired on Wednesday. The fellow who hired me was out of town Tuesday."
　　　　　—Nelson Algren, writer

"To survive there you need the ambition of a Latin American revolutionary, the ego of a grand opera tenor, and the physical stamina of a cow pony."
　　　　　—Billie Burke, actress

"Hollywood is like a world's fair that's been up a year too long."
　　　　　—Sonny Fox, actor

"Hollywood is a sewer—with service from the Ritz Carlton."
　　　　　—Wilson Mizner, playwright

"It's a shame to take this country away from the rattlesnakes."
　　　　　—D.W. Griffith, director

"They ruin your stories. They trample your pride. They massacre your ideas. And what do you get for it? A fortune."
　　　　　—anonymous

pack it in and go someplace safe, like Switzerland.

There, perhaps as therapy, he wrote a very funny, very angry letter to Hollywood. Its hero is a successful producer named Felix Farmer (Richard Mulligan), who has made hit after wholesome hit for Capitol Pictures but has also had to battle the cost-cutting, picture-slashing brass, personified by a reptilian David Blackman (Robert Vaughn), every inch of the way. When the nerve-frayed Felix makes the biggest flop in film history, a $30 million debacle called *Night Wind*, he cracks and attempts suicide at his Malibu beach house. No one, not his hedonistic hack of a director, Tim Culley (William Holden), not his scotch-and-Maalox-swigging press agent, Ben Coogan (Robert Weber), not his glib and decadent doctor, Irving Feingarten (Robert Preston), not even his wife, the squeaky-clean family-picture star Sally Miles (Julie Andrews, a.k.a. Edwards' wife) can snap him out of it.

It's only during an orgy at his home (through which he is medicated and catatonic), when a nubile starlet crawls beneath his blankets, that Felix comes to with a revelation that will save his picture and his career—turn G-rated *Night Wind* into a sex film! He is so possessed by this lunatic idea that he is willing to give up his shares in Capitol Pictures and put his family's every penny on the line just to finance the project, which soon requires his icon of a wife to do much more than sing. After a nude scene (for which she must be drugged), as Sally freaks at the prospect of losing both her reputation and all her assets, she tries to cut a deal of her own, thanks to the ministrations of her lawyer, Herb Moskowitz (Robert

Julie Andrews prepares to bare it all in this climatic scene from Blake Edward's S.O.B.

Loggia), her ambitious social secretary, Gary Murdock (Stuart Margolin), and her mountainous agent, Eva Brown (Shelley Winters). From here, it's an orgy of back-stabbing and more desperate acts, of not only the desperate diva, the demented, dedicated producer, and the various studio vermin, but a three-timing starlet (Marisa Berenson), a surly Chinese chef (Benson Fong), and a shrewish gossip columnist (Loretta Swit) falling into the fray.

The script was even nastier in its original form. By the time he had repatriated and had reawakened studio interest with two more hit *Pink Panther* sequels, as well as the libidinously laugh-rich *10* (1979), Edwards had mellowed his new script into marketability. But history repeated itself as Orion Pictures finally took on both S.O.B. and another Swiss script, *The Ferret* (in which Dudley Moore would play the bungling son of a an assassinated super-spy), and then scuttled both projects in 1979. Edwards later repeated his own spending history, building a lavish $500,000 house set in Malibu's Paradise Cove and orchestrating a $200,000 press junket (including airline tickets, hotel, supper at La Scala West, sweatshirts, catered poolside cabana interviews with the stars, and a dinner party at the Beverly Hills Hotel's Crystal Room), for which he ended up footing the bill. The distributors repeated history by originally gearing publicity for the film around Andrews' naked torso, causing Edwards to comment, "Clearly they perceive the film first as the baring of my wife's breasts and second as a comedy."

For all the foibles on every side, there isn't a truthful dig that this dark autobiographical "fairy tale" doesn't get in. After the "Once upon a time..." opening, the first thing we witness is a natty jogger (a seven-time Edwards film veteran, his personal physician, Herbert Tanney) keeling over from a coronary on the beach in front of Felix's house. There he remains throughout the entire movie as happy Angelenos ignore him, even with his dog howling over his corpse. So much for background.

Every single member of this sprawling ensemble does wickedly worthy work that even Robert Altman must have envied. Edwards called in a host of old friends and relations, from William Holden (*The Wild Rovers*, 1971) to Craig Stevens (star of Edwards' *Peter Gunn* television series) to his own daughter, Jennifer. Preston, Weber, and Holden are as vice-ridden and loyal a trio of buddies as any producer could wish for. As the deranged Felix, Richard Mulligan is no-holds-barred nuts. Holden later confessed Mulligan's effect on him: "For the first time in my life, I felt I was losing control in a scene."

Though the studio brass may have cleaned things up here and there (bull droppings were no longer piled on the poster's shiny title), *S.O.B.* gets away with murder (though not as outrageous as illuminating a scene with the light from John Ritter's glow-in-the-dark condom in the adulterous *Skin Deep*, 1979). As for the repercussions of holding the mirror up to Hollywood, Edwards can only say, "I want to tell you that various people are repeating lines straight out of the script." Super-agent Sue

Mengers put it more originally, after seeing a little too much of herself in Shirley Winters' Eva Brown: "An Alp should fall on his house."

Rock and Roll Animal!... or Is That "Enema"?

Not the Commitments, the Partridge Family, the Monkees, the Ruttles, not even the Blues Brothers started out like this. Christopher Guest (an Emmy-winning actor who plays seven different instruments and had long written satire for the *National Lampoon*) was hanging out in the lobby of Hollywood's notorious Chateau Marmont Hotel when he saw a stoned, over-the-hill English rock star insensibly wrangling with the front desk clerk over some lost luggage. Soon, Guest and his pal, songwriter and actor Michael McKean (who

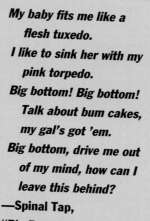

My baby fits me like a flesh tuxedo.
I like to sink her with my pink torpedo.
Big bottom! Big bottom!
Talk about bum cakes, my gal's got 'em.
Big bottom, drive me out of my mind, how can I leave this behind?
—Spinal Tap, "Big Bottom"

Rockumentarian Marti De Bergi (Rob Reiner at left) and metal rocker Nigel Tufnel (Christopher Guest) amid Nigel's cherished, if seldom played, guitars in **This Is Spinal Tap** *(1984).*

had toured extensively with Lenny and the Squigtones after his eight-year stint as a musical greaser on TV's *Laverne and Shirley*) were goofing on late-night cable shows as past-their-prime rockers Nigel Tufnel and David St. Hubbins, childhood bandmates from Squatney, England. McKean's pal Harry Shearer (a musician who also boasted a Grammy nomination for comedy record producing, and who was also a writing consultant for television's cult favorite *Fernwood Two Night*) got into the act as bass player Derek Smalls, from the small Midlands village of Nilford-on-Null (not far from Wolverhampton, if that places it for you).

One night, the multitalented trio found themselves on a TV show called *The T.V. Show* with friend Rob Reiner (former director of the improv troupe The Session and best known as Archie's son-in-law from *All in the Family*). While preparing to perform a skit that parodied interview segments from television's *Midnight Special* and "waiting for the machine that was supposed to make the fog effect to stop dripping oil on us," as Shearer remembers, the boys started playing their characters, and Reiner riffed along as Wolfman Jack, interviewing "one of England's loudest bands," a group called—a drum roll, please—Spinal Tap.

They had such a good time that soon every time the four got together socially, they'd talk Tap and flesh out the fantasy a little more. They created elaborate histories for all three band members. For instance, Derek had been the original bassist for England's pio-

> *It's weird when you get a piece of parody that's so far reaching that it nearly destroys an entire art form.*
> —Ian Astbury, of the heavy metal band The Cult

neer all-white Jamaican show band, Skaface. And in seventeen years, Nigel and David's bands had gone from the Originals to the New Originals to the Dutchmen, the Thamesmen, Rave Breakers, Shiners, Mondos, Doppel Gang, People's Loose Lips, Waffles, Hot Waffles, Silver Service, Mud Below, the Tufnel St. Hubbins' Group, and finally to Spinal Tap.

Next, the instruments and staff paper came out and eleven tasteless tunes were penned and practiced to perfection. Though at first they toyed with punk, they went with the metal sound—"a more stationary target...when you're working on a film that won't come out for three years," said Shearer. "Sex Farm Woman," "Hell Hole," "Tonight, I'm Gonna Rock You Tonight," "Big Bottom," "Intravenus De Milo," and others became rock realities, as Reiner, Guest, McKean, and Shearer thought out a basic story for Spinal Tap's less-than-triumphant American tour, a tour where everything that could possibly go wrong would. With some seed money, they

BELOW: Bassist Derek Smalls is smaller than we thought and airport security is about to earn its pay in This Is Spinal Tap (1984). OPPOSITE: Are you ready to rock? Are you ready to roll in the aisles? Meet (from left to right) David St. Hubbins (Michael McKean), Mick Shrimpton (R.J. Parnell), Nigel Tufnel (Christopher Guest), Viv Savage (David Kaff), and Derek Smalls (Harry Shearer)—otherwise known as Spinal Tap.

A large majority of the reviews don't talk about Chris's or Mike's or Harry's acting or the direction. The film is so seamless, they don't think anybody's acting in it or directing it—as if it just sort of happened. To me, that's a compliment.
—Rob Reiner, on *This Is Spinal Tap* (1984)

put sample footage together of Marti Di Bergi's (Rob Reiner taking a loving potshot at *The Last Waltz'* director, Martin Scorsese) rockumentary about Spinal Tap. Armed with no script and just twenty minutes of wild yet convincing videotape, Reiner and documentary producer Karen Murphy shopped the project around and sold it to Embassy Pictures.

After the green light, Spinal Tap's world became more populated. They needed a host of secondary characters to fill their satire. Keyboards could be handled by Viv Savage (David Kaff, who had recorded with Chuck Berry, The Average White Band, and King Crimson). Mick Shrimpton (R.J. Parnell, who had drummed for Engelbert Humperdinck) would be the latest in a series of percussionists who keep exploding and expiring. Ian Faith (former *National Lampoon* editor Tony Hendra) would be the apple-cheeked, not-quite-on-the-ball road manager to lead their U.S. invasion.

Love interest? Besides countless "special friends" (a.k.a. groupies), there would be Jeanine Pettibone (June Chadwick), David's astrologer, dressed "like an Australian nightmare," ready to join the tour and cause all sorts of internal strife. The boys' label would be Polymer Records, commanded by the fatuous Sir Dennis Eton Hogg (Patrick McNee) and liaisoned by a nasal-voiced, foul-mouthed vamp named Bobbi Fleckman (the incomparably crass Fran Drescher). They would even have a limo driver (Bruno Kirby) on tour, whose idea of good music was Frank Sinatra. Other

No performance nightmares for these blokes. Spinal Tap are a performance nightmare. Nigel Tufnel (Christopher Guest) displays some expert heavy metal posturing.

cameos would include Dana Carvey, Billy Crystal, Angelica Huston, Fred Willard, Howard Hessman, Paul Benedict, and Ed Begley, Jr.

The writers mapped out each hilarious mishap that might befall their befuddled band on its "Smell the Glove" tour. The band would somehow skip Boston entirely. They would manage to lose their way to the stage in the basement of a Cleveland arena. They would get wrangled into a record signing that nobody shows up for in Chicago by promoter Artie Pupkin (David Letterman's maestro, Paul Schaffer). They'd get snubbed by bigger bands and their managers. They would cancel in Memphis and sing off-key around Elvis' grave. They'd take flak in Atlanta for their *Smell the Glove* record cover of a naked, oiled woman on all fours on a leash with a black glove stuck in her face. Their awesome Stonehenge set would run into hilarious complications in Austin. In Seattle, they would be booked into a military base's dinner dance as Spinal Tarp. The list of screw-ups was virtually endless.

With their chops down and some semblance of a scenario, Spinal Tap next hit the concert scene. Opening at Radio City in Anaheim, California, for Killer Pussy (whose big hit was "Teenage

Enema Nurse in Bondage"), they were applauded, much to their amazement. When slated to open for Iron Butterfly at Gazzari's Night Club in Los Angeles, that band's drummer had a toothache, and Spinal Tap waited through "In-a-Gadda-Da-Vida" (with "three identical guitar solos," according to Shearer), then went on and "played alarmingly loud and nobody noticed we weren't a so-called real band. That's when we knew we were ready to start filming."

Reiner was more than ready. He'd rounded up some real rock-and-roll talent to help fake his cinema vérité. His director of photography had shot parts of the fabled *Gimme Shelter*. Lights for the concert footage were designed by the band Boston's lighting pro and operated by the company that lit Rod Stewart, Queen, Ted Nugent, and the Go-Gos. His set designer worked for Eddie Money and Santana. His sound crew was ready to make sure that, unlike in most concerts, fans understood every syllable sung.

There would be no wink-wink-nudge-nudge commentary for *This Is Spinal Tap* (1984)—just a bird's-eye view of an enterprise coming unglued. Reiner filmed the almost wholly improvised dialogue for each scene and interview without a break (except for technical screw-ups), then reshot them to see if anything fresh would arise. Through it all, the delightful cluelessness of McKean's, Guest's, and Shearer's richly detailed characters is depicted with wicked subtlety. As Nigel Tufnel deeply and dimly notes, "There's such a fine line between clever and stupid." From a very human embarrassment with an airport metal detector to pyrotechnically malfunctioning sets, this satire is razor sharp.

Perhaps the funniest moment in the film is when Nigel plays a surprisingly classical, mellow, and melodic piano piece for Marti (having already taken him on a tour of his sacred guitar and amp collection). Hands flowing across the ivories, Nigel confesses that what he's playing is "part of a trilogy I'm writing. I've always been influenced by Mozart and Bach." When the awestruck Marti asks the name

of the pretty piece, without missing a note, Nigel responds, "What's it called? 'Lick My Love Pump.' "

This Is Spinal Tap was a smash—and led to a nationwide concert tour for the band, two albums, called *Spinal Tap* and *Break Like the Wind*, and a popular CD-ROM. With fifty hours of film and no script, it's no wonder that Reiner and his editor had their work cut out for them slicing up this slice of life. It's only too bad that we can't see the other forty-eight hours.

The Best Is Yet to Come

There are a lot of iconoclasts still sitting in the back row and making life just a little funnier (and more hellish) for those of us who think we've got our acts together. The nineties are already affording ample fuel to fan these comedic fires of rage that promise to touch off every tinder in sight, from trendy Contract with America politics (*Bob Roberts*, 1992) to the glam fashion industry (*Prêt-à-Porter* [*Ready to Wear*], 1994) to the ultimate sacred institution so much more cherished since the O.J. Simpson trial (*Jury Duty*, 1995). Maybe nothing really is sacred, but as veteran satirist Eric Idle once pointed out, "One way of measuring the freedom of any society is the amount and style of comedy that's allowed. A healthy society allows more satirical comment than a repressive one, so if comedy is to act as a safety valve, it has to deal with taboos."

God bless America. Now about that Mother Theresa movie...

He's young, Republican, and damn proud of being shallow. Folk singer turned politician Bob Roberts was the title character in Tim Robbins' scathing debut as a director.

Chapter Six

YOU'RE A BIG GENRE NOW

If I have seen further, it is by standing on the shoulders of giants.

—Sir Isaac Newton

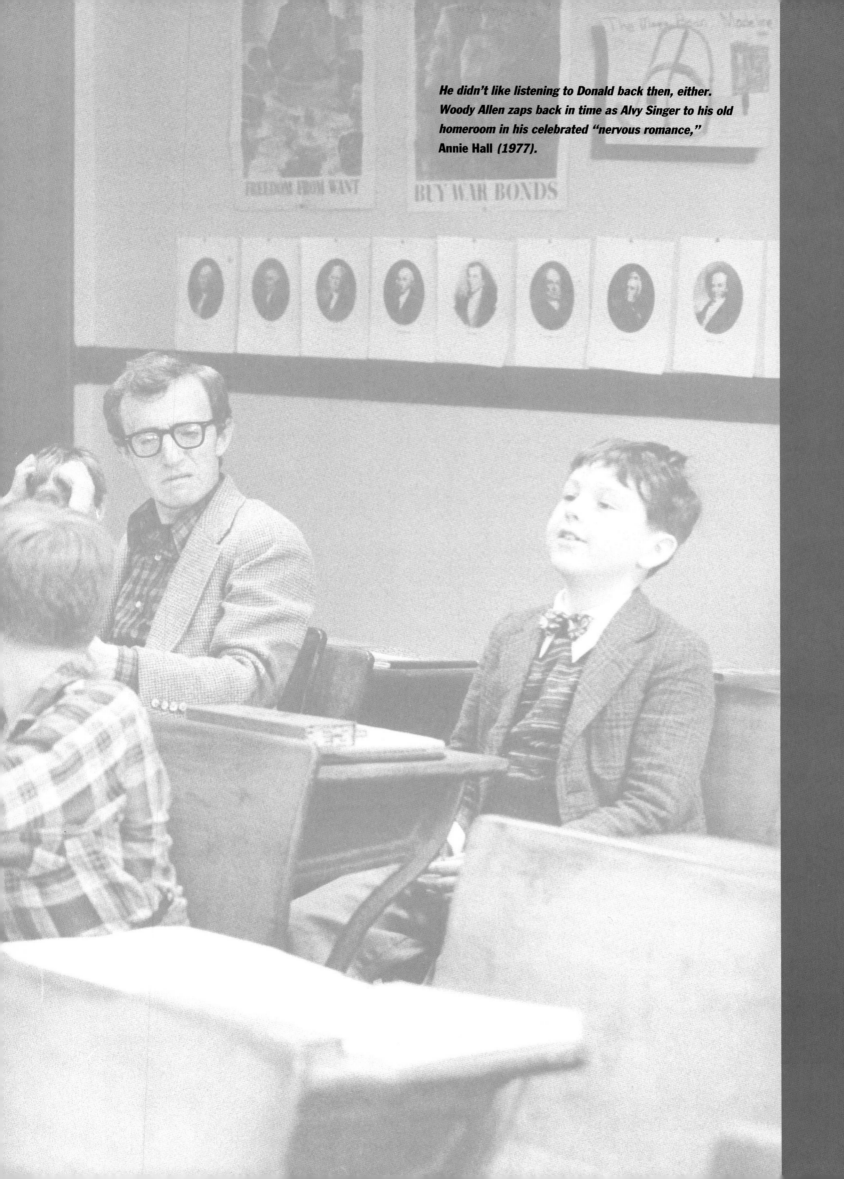

He didn't like listening to Donald back then, either. Woody Allen zaps back in time as Alvy Singer to his old homeroom in his celebrated "nervous romance," Annie Hall (1977).

The following is a condensed debate. The names have been changed to protect the nonexistent.

YOUTH: Comedy is so fresh now! Talk about ancient history—your man Buster Keaton wore his first diapers a hundred years ago.

EXPERIENCE: Yes, and the same town that lures you and your friends to the mall with *Hot Shots: Part Deux* (1993) recently rolled out the red carpet for several gala centenary tributes for the old dude, complete with black-and-white birthday cake.

YOUTH: Well, you can't say that anyone has gotten a custard pie in the face for about eighty years.

EXPERIENCE: Didn't John Belushi get a whole college cafeteria in the face in *Animal House* (1978)?

YOUTH: Yeah, but you have to admit that it's almost a lifetime since any hokey runaway brides left their grooms at the altar while they took off with some funny poor guy.

EXPERIENCE: You're right. Now it's grooms who wreak matrimonial havoc, like that drunk Dudley Moore in *Arthur* (1981) and that oh-so-proper Hugh Grant in *Four Weddings and a Funeral* (1994).

YOUTH: Well, at least I know that acting like an overgrown, spastic idiot isn't as acceptable in movies as it was in the 1950s with Jerry Lewis.

EXPERIENCE: Would that be an idiot like *Tommy Boy* (1995), *Billy Madison* (1995), *Ernest Goes to Jail* (1990), or *Dumb and Dumber* (1994)...in the words of Jim Carrey, "Somebody stop me!"

YOUTH: Okay! So maybe movies aren't so fresh.

Maybe they are. Ultimately, comedy is a cumulative art, one that, if it doesn't always respect its elders, is at least happy to steal from them. If provocateur Sam Kinnison could have stretched his greasy paw back across the decades to slap five with Lenny Bruce,

so Paul Reiser might have thrown a wink across town to legend George Burns. As Bette Midler has sometimes seemed a more buoyant Mae West, Cheech and Chong could have bumbled into Abbott and Costello in any number of films (reefer excluded).

Today, for all the interchangeable television sitcoms that are targeted at white-bread yuppie twenty-somethings, the playing field for film funniness is broader than ever, running in age groups from Macaulay Culkin's films and *Look Who's Talking Too* (1990) all the way up to Jessica Tandy's classy *Camilla* (1995) or Paul Newman's working-class *Nobody's Fool* (1994). From the cute *Babe* (1995), the talking pig, to Spike Lee's confrontational and political comedies, no one style reigns supreme. From family values to sex, violence, and even introspection, all topics are fair game for laughs. The best of today's comedies all have two things: the willingness to push the laugh envelope, exploring what can be considered funny, and a commitment from their writers and directors to artistic growth.

Woody Takes a Long Hard Look at Love

His movies were always funny, but they weren't always sophisticated. "The closest analogy to my films would be the Tom and Jerry cartoons," Woody Allen has said. "A guy runs out and you smash

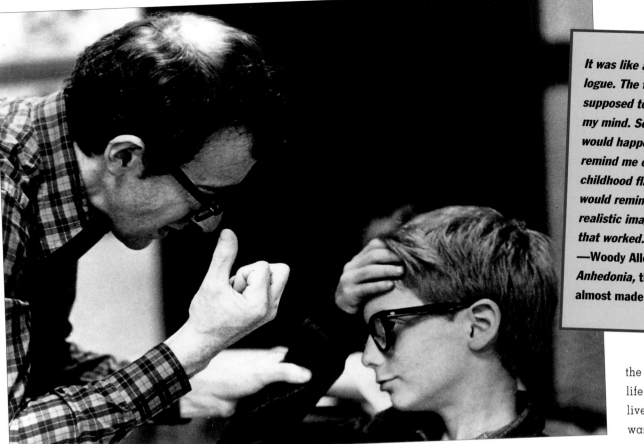

How often do you get to lecture yourself? Alvy Singer (Woody Allen) wrangles with young Alvy (Jonathan Munk) in Annie Hall.

him on the head with something and he doesn't die and he doesn't bleed and it's fast and you clear the decks for the next joke right away.... My films certainly lack depth." Whether clowning around in the futuristic *Sleeper* (1973) or "Russian" around in the period send-up *Love and Death* (1976), Allen's performing persona as the angst-ridden, overarticulate nebbish was always clear. What wasn't clear was just how he really felt about things. His rise to becoming America's most cherished comedy director was spurred by a 1977 film that, but for some radical rethinking in the cutting room, would have borne little resemblance to the classic we now know as the "nervous romance," *Annie Hall* (1977).

This bittersweet saga of the rise and fall and rise and ultimate fall of death-obsessed, dyed-in-the-wool-neurotic New York stand-up comic Alvy Singer's romance with a goofily beguiling, beautiful, suit-wearing, pot-smoking, aspiring nightclub singer from Wisconsin named Annie Hall won an unprecedented four Oscars for directing, screenplay, actress, and picture. It broke new ground in romantic comedy, but not before it almost broke its own neck.

After his Russian romp, Allen had wanted to do a personal movie, and thus he began filming *Anhedonia* (a psychiatric term for the inability to experience pleasure). According to longtime cowriter Marshall Brickman, *Anhedonia* was first conceived as "the story of a guy who lived in New York and was forty years old and examining his life. His life consisted of several strands. One was a relationship with a young woman, another was a concern for

the banality of the life that we all live, and a third was an obsession with proving himself and testing himself to find out what kind of character he had."

The plot was so personal that there was hardly room for romance at all. In the space of six weeks, Allen and his crew shot ten thousand feet (3,048m), or more than forty hours, of film. Annie Hall (Diane Keaton, whose real name is Diane Hall) made a brief appearance at the top of the film and disappeared in much of the rest of it while Alvy's flashbacks and lurid fantasies took precedence. Here are a few of the changes we would have seen in *Anhedonia*.

What Woody Whittled Away

Remember Alvy's Brooklyn family who lived under the roller coaster at Coney Island? We would have seen Alvy's mother kvetching, "It's not the same now that the element have moved in," to which a time-tripping Alvy would respond, "The element, can you believe that? My mother was always worried that 'the element' would move in. It's like a science-fiction movie." From there, we'd have seen a sci-fi segment about an invading African-American family from outer space.

Remember the grade-school flashback where the little tykes tell the camera where they'll be in thirty-five years? (One kid says, "I used to be a heroin addict. Now I'm a methadone addict." Another twinkles, "I'm into leather.") We would have seen Alvy follow one classmate, Donald, the model student, into his adult life as the president of "a profitable dress company." After berating him for everything from letting his children memorize television commercials to living a predictable and boring existence, he would even criticize what his television was playing and would debate with the game-show host on the screen. (Host: "What do you mean, this is the worst kind of show? This show is very popular. We give away a lot of prizes—that's fun!")

Remember young Alvy (played by Jonathan Munk), who has to put up with Joey Nichols, the family friend whose idea of relating to a kid is pressing a coin into his forehead? We would have seen young Alvy sitting beneath the Coney Island boardwalk getting a condom from a friend ("When I was ten, I knew I should carry around an emergency contraceptive"). From there we'd flash to a teenage Alvy and his girlfriend fooling around under the boardwalk as he takes the vintage condom out of his wallet ("By the time I got to use it, it was dust").

In another flashback, we would have seen young Alvy cooking his thermometer on the radiator so that his voluptuous cousin Doris ("Alvy, you're drooling!") would come over and read him comic books about Hitler. We would then cut to a fantasy where the older Alvy is testing his courage as a WWII French resistance fighter. Captured by the Gestapo, his compatriot Jean-Paul Sartre has refused to talk and has been executed. Alvy stands firm, saying, "Because of my moral convictions, I cannot name names." Taking a hand puppet out of his pocket, he adds, "But he can," and tells all.

Later, we would have seen Alvy and Pam (Shelly Duvall as the *Rolling Stone* reporter to whom sex with Alvy is a Kafka-esque experience) transported from a transcendent happening for the Maharishi at Yankee Stadium ("Look, there's God coming out of the bathroom") to the Garden of Eden, where they rap with God about sex, anatomy, and the myth of the female orgasm.

Remember Annie's waspy, ham-passing family (with Colleen Dewhurst as Mom and Christopher Walken as brother Duane, who likes to imagine running head-on into highway traffic)? We would have seen Mom Hall taking snapshots of everyone after dinner when she recalls a funny dream she's had the night before, in which she had a fight with a man over who had control of the television ("It was not Dad, Annie, but he was wearing your dad's bathrobe"). She got furious and snapped off the television antenna, and when the man asked for it back, she ran upstairs and flushed it down the toilet. When she asks Alvy how his analyst would interpret it, he stammers, "You're kidding me."

We would have also seen a ten- to fifteen-minute sequence of Annie, Alvy, and his childhood pal Rob's (Tony Roberts) time-trip back to Alvy's Brooklyn home, where his parents acted as waspy as Annie's. (Dad: "Make me a martini." Mom: "Of course, sweetheart. How would you like it, dear?" Dad: "On white bread with mayonnaise.") We would then have cut to the Devil himself taking the trio on an elevator tour through the nine layers of hell ("Layer

five: organized crime, fascist dictators, and people who don't appreciate oral sex").

Remember Alvy dragging Marshall McLuhan onscreen to settle a debate with a puffed-up professor over a movie line? In *Anhedonia*, the media master stuck around to discuss Alvy's college days and the shame of being brought before a dean for burning an effigy of another dean.

Remember Alvy's love affair with Los Angeles ("a city where the only cultural advantage is turning right on a red light")? We would have seen a zombielike Rob greet Annie and Alvy upon their arrival with prepared sleeping pods for them ("When you sleep, they will take over your bodies and you will become happy citizens of L.A.").

> *Woody Allen is America's Ingmar Bergman....It's about time that we recognized Woody Allen as one of our most personal, passionate, most introspective filmmakers....I haven't seen an American film in years that was as seriously interested in the relations between men and women as Annie Hall.*
> —Vincent Canby, on the film Woody did make

Streamlining

In the editing room, Allen, Brickman, and editor Ralph Rosenblum were faced with a picture that, as Brickman said, "was running off in nine different directions." Out came the red pencil. Almost all of the first twenty minutes were lopped off in order to establish Keaton's wonderful Annie more quickly. Brickman admitted he felt like "the flesh was being ripped from my body," but with so much footage to choose from, a simpler love story was patched together.

New shots had to be added to keep it making sense. Why was Alvy going out to Los Angeles, for instance? To fill the gap that a deleted rant against Tinseltown had left, Allen added a scene that brought him the biggest laugh he had ever had in a film. He and Annie discuss their plans for the coast while snorting coke with some Manhattan friends. Purely by accident, Allen sneezes while examining a box containing $2,000 worth of the precious powder, resulting in a cloud of white that no audience will ever forget. As Rosenblum remembers, "The laughter was so great at each of our test screenings that I kept having to add more and more feet of dead film to keep the laughter from pushing the next scene off the screen." Watching the film, you can see Keaton covering her mouth to keep from laughing herself.

Almost every comic moment was now shared between Alvy and Annie, interweaving flashbacks, flashforwards, confessional commentary, and even cartoons from their lives together and apart. From his heroic rescue of her from spiders in the bathtub ("Darling, I've been killing spiders since I was thirty") to squeamishly chasing live lobsters from behind the refrigerator ("Maybe if I put a little dish of butter sauce here with a nutcracker, it will run out the other side"), it was love. Allen still wanted to keep the original title for this love story. Brickman suggested playful alternatives: *A Roller Coaster Named Desire*, *Me and My Goy*, and (in honor of one of Keaton's songs in the film and of Allen's fear of anti-

guy goes to a psychiatrist and says, "Doc, my brother's crazy. He thinks he's a chicken." And the doctor says, "Well, why don't you turn him in?" And the guy says, "I would, but I need the eggs." Well, I guess that's pretty much how I feel about relationships. You know, they're totally irrational and crazy and absurd...but I guess we keep goin' through it because most of us need the eggs.

Less Is More, or...Peter Sellers Finds out Why He Isn't Dead

You know the show-biz story of how when a performer really gets "hot," he's often offered every role under the sun, from old ladies to Manchurian warlords? Well, there was one actor who earned such crazy confidence: Peter Sellers, regarded by many as the greatest comic actor who ever lived.

Born into a music-hall family and discovering his own chameleon character inclinations at age twenty in the RAF's entertainment unit during World War II, Sellers got his start in English radio by calling up a BBC producer and bogusly recommending himself in the voices of two leading radio personalities. Work with radio's legendary Spike Milligan on *The Goon Show* led to a movie break with character master Alec Guinness in the Ealing Studios' black comedy *The Lady Killers* (1955) (where he gave the cast gifts of mock interviews with them—Sellers playing their parts, of course). By the time of his noncomic performance as an irascible shop steward in the labor union story *I'm All Right, Jack* (1959), Sellers was a major star and had won the British Best Actor Oscar over Sir Laurence Olivier.

Sellers was so brilliantly funny in *The Pink Panther* (1963) that Blake Edwards started filming its sequel, *A Shot in the Dark* (1964), before the first film was even released. Mel Brooks tried to woo the actor into *The Producers* (1968) while tagging along on a shopping trip through Bloomingdale's. On one of his first trips to America, Sellers was offered no fewer than twenty-five screen roles. His ship had come in. With each new film, Sellers seemed to metamorphose into a totally convincing and usually hilarious character (and sometimes several). Yet he was a deeply troubled man who believed that he had no character of his own. Then, at 4:32 A.M. on April 7, 1964, the character issue died...and so did Peter Sellers, at least momentarily. A series of heart attacks (thirteen, to be exact) stopped his heart for ninety seconds. The "deceased" Sellers had an out-of-body experience, and while floating overhead, he saw the attempts to resuscitate him. He was drawn toward a light, yet drawn more strongly back into his body. When he awoke, he was plagued by the question of why he had been sent back to earth. With all he had accomplished, what had he been saved for?

> **To see me as a person on the screen is one of the dullest experiences you could experience.**
> **—Peter Sellers**

Inspector Clouseau (Peter Sellers) just wants someone to spar with in the immensely popular The Pink Panther *(1963).*

Semitism) *It Had to Be Jew.* But *Anhedonia* would have needed an expensive ad campaign just to convince potential viewers that it wasn't a Balkan documentary. After Woody toyed with *Anxiety and Annie and Alvy*, he settled on the film's new focus, *Annie Hall*.

Allen also tried several endings to wrap up the film. In one, Alvy obsessively placed phone calls—that were unreturned—across the country to Annie. In another, he got reattached but couldn't fall out of love with Annie. Finally, Rosenblum bluntly urged him to shoot one where he told the audience how much he missed her and what a mistake it was to leave her. Alvy did, once more stopping strangers in the street to get their input, but that still didn't end the picture. Rosenblum suggested that Allen go back to his opening monologue with its Groucho joke ("I would never want to belong to a club that would have someone like me for a member") for his answer. It didn't gel until the cab ride to the studio to shoot it. Allen would end his loving paean to the tangle of human hearts with another theft from the past. He told Rosenblum that he would wing it when he got there, and he did. It went like this:

> *It was great seeing Annie again....I realized what a terrific person she was and how much fun it was just knowing her and I thought of that old joke, you know, the*

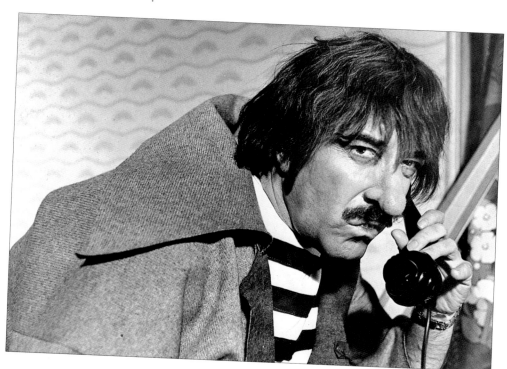

RIGHT: Collect call for Quasimodo. Just one of the supersleuth's oh-so-clever disguises in The Pink Panther Strikes Again (1976). BELOW: Clouseau goes undercover as he hunts for a murderess in the first pink sequel, A Shot in the Dark (1964).

The answer came in 1971, during a slump in his career, when he read the novella *Being There* by Polish author Jerzy Kosinski, about a dim-witted child-man, a gardener named Chauncey "Chance" Gardiner. Its simple hero is ejected from the house that he has never set foot out of, after the death of his lifelong employer. All Chance knows is the television he watches and continually mimics, and his plants. After wandering the streets of New York, he is slightly injured by the limousine of Eve Rand, wife of America's most powerful industrialist, the elderly and dying Benjamin Rand. Chance's journey into the Rands' palatial home and to the inner circles of the power elite is a magical one, for his intensity and openness are

mistaken for much more. His sound-byte memory and what director Hal Ashby calls "a childlike aura" leave him, and,as Kosinski puts it, he becomes" devoid of any particular will that might trigger a negative reaction." Quite unintentionally, Chauncey Gardiner finds himself upwardly mobile in the extreme.

Sellers instinctively knew that this tabula rasa of a role was what he was destined for. Kosinski received an anonymous telegram reading: "Available, my garden or outside it. C. Gardiner." Intrigued, the author called an attached telephone number and listened to the movie star's pitch in amazement, and the seeds were sewn for the film version of *Being There* (1979).

Kosinski's book was inspired by three things: the gardener in Shakespeare's *Richard II*, who uses horticultural terms for the political arena; a study that showed that college grads in the late 1960s had already logged in an average of eighteen thousand hours of television (equal to about nine years of a steady job); and the increasing importance to political candidates of a sincere media image. Though he wanted the role of Chance for himself, over the next several years Sellers wooed him, pretending to be Chance at any party they both attended (moving guests out of his line of view of any television in sight), wrote to him as Chance, telephoned him as Chance, and finally, in the Malibu garden of a mutual friend, gardened as that gardener. Before the author's eyes, the normally swinging Sellers became older and stiffer. "His face was utterly serene," Kosinski recalls. "It was as if I wasn't within a hundred miles. He had stepped into his own world. He was my Chauncey Gardiner."

In 1973, Sellers first approached Hal Ashby to direct. He had greatly admired Ashby's *Harold and Maude* (1971), a darkly comic love story between an adolescent Bud Cort and a wizened Ruth Gordon. Neither Sellers nor Ashby alone had the clout to get a movie as weird as *Being There* made, so it wasn't until after Sellers' triumphs in the *Pink Panther* sequels and Ashby's popular *Shampoo* (1975) and triumphant *Coming Home* (1978) that the green light lit.

An Actor Prepares

As Ashby's production crew transformed the Biltmore House (Cornelius Vanderbilt's 250-room estate on ten thousand wooded acres [4,047ha] in North Carolina) into the Rand mansion in the new locale of Washington, D.C., Sellers went through a challenge even more monumental. Suffering from attacks of tachycardia (in which his heart sped up to as many as 110 beats a minute) and fearing a final heart attack at any moment, he found himself searching for the character he had fought so hard to claim. As he later said, "I'd often thought of him over the years, but when I actually had to play Chance, I realized I didn't know what he looked like or how he spoke."

What to do with a character who, when the FBI has his voice analyzed, comes out without any trace of an identifiable accent? How to play a blank slate without being boring? The obsessed Sellers went to work. As his wife, Lynne Fredericks, recalled, "Peter tried out a whole continent of American accents, which I taped and played back." One would be too southern, another too West Coast, another too New York. "To listen to Peter's repeated efforts," she added, "was a little like watching a man unpacking a travel bag [and looking] for something he fears he hasn't packed."

Salvation came from Sellers' study wall. From abode to abode, the actor had brought a huge, framed blowup of his early comedy idol, Stan Laurel. That was it! Soon, Fredericks had set up a video-camera and was filming Sellers walking, sitting, eating, and talking with a clearly enunciated American twist on Laurel's simplicity. A heavier, less flexible, almost primitive way of moving started to give Chance a distinct physical life. Sellers put on weight because Chance was, in his view, "sedentary and solitary, even eats like a big child, which is basically what he is." He let his hair go gray and asked Lynne to coif it into the monastic crew cut that Chance's housekeeper, Louise, might have given him. When Sellers walked onto the set, he was Chance.

OPPOSITE: An early moment for Seller's crowning character, the child-man Chance the gardener, in Being There (1979). RIGHT: The newly dubbed Chauncey Gardiner is moving up in the world thanks to socialite Eve Rand (Shirley MacLaine) in Being There.

Aside from telling spiritual costar Shirley MacLaine about his metaphysical experience while the two filmed their first marathon scene together in the back of a limousine, Sellers kept to himself—he didn't want to break character on the mammoth set (so vast that for two months it housed Ashby's one hundred-plus crew, production offices, and design shops). His commitment paid off in a character so innocent and otherworldly that despite *Being There* being an undeniably slow-paced comedy, it is never anything but riveting.

Chance is unlike anything the master comedian had ever done—simplicity itself. Sellers' seriousness when it comes to Chance's integrity and complete openness makes him as comical as he is touching in his almost unearthly situation. From getting hit on by a gay politico at a Washington party to being threatened with a switchblade by a D.C. gang leader, Chance has a childlike aura that works. "What astounded me was the reductive quality of Peter's gestures," admitted Kosinski. "He had the kinetic restriction of children who watch television excessively—abandoned, so to speak, to the loneliness of their private garden."

Unfortunately, *Being There* didn't earn Sellers the Oscar that he had hoped for, though it did get Melvyn Douglas an award for Best Supporting Actor for his heartfelt yet tough-as-nails tycoon. Against Sellers' protests, Ashby had added outtakes to the final credits of the actor cracking up while trying to deliver the slang-filled message that he had promised a gang leader to deliver to someone named Raphael. Relaying it to the first African-American man he sees, in this case a doctor who is examining him, Sellers' Chance couldn't quite get out the silly words...take after giggle-

filled take. While audiences now salivate to see this master in a candid moment, in 1979 it broke the spell of a character whose otherworldly energy had carried an entire film. Dustin Hoffman may have won the Oscar for *Kramer vs. Kramer* (1979) that year (a role he could have done in his sleep), but Sellers' more offbeat humanity made the minimalist masterpiece of *Being There* his ultimate reason for being here.

Other Dummies

Since Chance said "I like to watch," we have enjoyed several more super-simple comedy performances worth mentioning. Among the best are Joe Morton's mild-mannered, mute alien experiencing his own marvelous misinterpretations by earthlings in John Sayles' *The Brother from Another Planet* (1984). Johnny Depp's hedge-snipping *Edward Scissorhands* (1990) cut straight to our alienated hearts, thanks to director Tim Burton. Mercedes Ruehl's dippy woman-child, Bella Kurnitz, in Neil Simon's loving look back at bygone Brooklyn, *Lost in Yonkers* (1993), was the finest female portrayal of that year. But perhaps most brilliant is Tom Hanks' big-hearted *Forrest Gump* (1994), which has had the chance to dazzle without any intellectual razzle.

This phenomenal, special effects–filled amble through American history by director Robert Zemeckis grossed $140 million in just twenty-eight days but was just as challenging to its star as *Being There* was to Sellers. As Hanks recalls, "The intensity of Forrest was even greater [than normal], because you have to stay stock-still, but the engine inside is still fully stoked; it's just going. It's harder to stay completely reined in than it is to come in and just chat, chat, chat." Yet chat he had to. To play the 75–I.Q.'d Gump

ABOVE: *Life* **is** *like a box of chocolates when you've received your second Oscar. Tom Hanks as the main character in* **Forrest Gump** *(1994).* **BELOW:** *Johnny Depp displays a little "handiwork" as the innocent* **Edward Scissorhands** *(1990).*

(screenwriter Winston Groom had chosen the surname Gump from a pile of his junk mail—a letter from Gump's Exclusive Jewelers in San Francisco), Hanks had to go "way character." He confesses, "I was very wary of the whole vocal thing, because it's not my gig; I don't know how to do it. I was always trying to convince Bob that there was some way of soft-pedaling it somehow." Luckily, he stuck it out, and his breakthrough came not from an old master but the mouths of babes— or one babe, seven-year-old Michael Humphries (young Forrest), to be exact. Humphries' goofy Mississippi drawl was just the inspiration Hanks needed to make "My Mama always says stupid is as stupid does" sound natural and win him his second consecutive Best Actor Oscar. Playing stupid is pretty smart.

A HAM BY ANY OTHER NAME

Okay, so you say you're smarter than Forrest. Let's see what kind of head you've got for names. The following lists of forty comedy stars are identical...except that one contains the names they were born with and the other contains the Hollywood monikers they were sold with. To give you an edge, we've added some films to the list. See how many you can match up.

REAL NAME	FILM	REEL NAME
1) Louis Francis Cristillo	Hold That Ghost (1941)	A) Doris Day
2) Elizabeth Edith Enke	The Apartment (1960)	B) Cary Grant
3) John Florence Sullivan	Love Thy Neighbor (1941)	C) Martha Raye
4) Allen Stewart Konigsberg	Casino Royale (1978)	D) Woody Allen
5) Eunice Quedens	At the Circus (1939)	E) George Burns
6) Frances Gumm	Easter Parade (1948)	F) Gene Wilder
7) Benjamin Kubelsky	To Be or Not to Be (1942)	G) Mickey Rooney
8) Melvin Kaminsky	Blazing Saddles (1974)	H) Whoopi Goldberg
9) Nathan Birnbaum	The Big Broadcast (1938)	I) Jack Oakie
10) Edward Israel Iskowitz	Kid Millions (1934)	J) Marie Dressler
11) Joe Yule, Jr.	The Human Comedy (1943)	K) Danny Kaye
12) Doris Van Kappelhoff	The Pajama Game (1957)	L) W.C. Fields
13) Alexandra Zuck	Romanoff and Juliet (1962)	M) Elliot Gould
14) Jeremiah Schwartz	It's a Mad, Mad, Mad, Mad World (1963)	N) Marilyn Monroe
15) Harris Glenn Milstead	Pink Flamingos (1972)	O) Divine
16) Lelia Von Koerber	Dinner at Eight (1933)	P) Andy Devine
17) William Claude Dukenfield	Poppy (1936)	Q) Michael Keaton
18) Karen Johnson	Made in America (1993)	R) Edie Adams
19) Elliot Goldstein	Getting Straight (1970)	S) Eddie Cantor
20) Archibald Leach	Once Upon a Honeymoon (1942)	T) Judy Garland
21) Leonard Hacker	The Love Bug (1969)	U) Jean Harlow
22) Joseph Levitch	Ladies' Man (1961)	V) Jerry Lewis
23) Paul Reubens	The Blues Brothers (1980)	W) Mel Brooks
24) Virginia McMath	Oh, Men, Oh, Women (1957)	X) Pee-Wee Herman
25) Jane Alice Peters	Rumba (1934)	Y) Buddy Hackett
26) Ruby Stevens	The Mad Miss Manton (1938)	Z) Carole Lombard
27) Jerry Silberman	The Adventure of Sherlock Holmes' Smarter Brother (1975)	AA) Walter Matthau
28) Harlean Carpenter	Saratoga (1937)	BB) Tony Randall
29) Judith Tuvim	Adam's Rib (1949)	CC) Fred Allen
30) David Daniel Kaminsky	The Inspector General (1949)	DD) Lou Costello
31) Michael Douglas	Much Ado About Nothing (1993)	EE) Ginger Rogers
32) Irving Lahrheim	The Night They Raided Minsky's (1968)	FF) Stan Laurel
33) Stanley Jefferson	The Flying Deuces (1939)	GG) Barbara Stanwyck
34) Walter Matuschankausky	A New Leaf (1971)	HH) Ed Wynn
35) Norma Jean Mortenson	Monkey Business (1952)	II) Judy Holliday
36) Leonard Rosenberg	Will Success Spoil Rock Hunter? (1957)	JJ) Jack Benny
37) Lewis Delaney Offield	The Great Dictator (1940)	KK) Eve Arden
38) Margaret Teresa Yvonne O'Reed	Monsieur Verdoux (1947)	LL) Sandra Dee

Answers: 1=DD, 2=R, 3=CC, 4=D, 5=KK, 6=T, 7=JJ, 8=W, 9=E, 10=S, 11=G, 12=A, 13=LL, 14=P, 15=O, 16=J, 17=L, 18=H, 19=M, 20=B, 21=Y, 22=V, 23=X, 24=EE, 25=Z, 26=GG, 27=F, 28=U, 29=II, 30=K, 31=Q, 32=HH, 33=FF, 34=AA, 35=N, 36=BB, 37=I, 38=C

What a Day This Has Been...

Metaphysics hasn't exactly been a staple of screen comedy over the years. Examining the nature of man's soul, let alone going into limbo to do it, is the kind of task you'd likely trust to only one man: Bill Murray. Of all the comedians to come down the pike since W.C. Fields, none has had the irreverent and unpredictable nature or the throwaway delivery that this former Chicagoan, Second City improv star, and *Saturday Night Live* superstar has perfected.

He's disrespected summer camp counselors in *Meatballs* (1979), gophers and golfers in *Caddyshack* (1980), Tarzan in *Shame*

> I can't make Bill do the script. I can't make him do anything. There's a great sigh of relief when he actually comes to the set.
> —director Harold Ramis, on Bill Murray, the star of his metaphysical *Groundhog Day* (1993)

of the Jungle (1980), Nixon while playing Hunter S. Thompson in *Where the Buffalo Roam* (1980), the U.S. Army in *Stripes* (1981), aspiring playwrights writing about Love Canal in *Tootsie* (1982), Charles Dickens in *Scrooged* (1988), bank robbers and clowns in *Quick Change* (1990), the entire field of psychotherapy in *What About Bob?* (1991), and the Mafia in *Mad Dog and Glory* (1993). Murray's quirky, highly improvisational style represents, in the words of director Harold Ramis, "a kind of shambling irony; he's heroic and disreputable at the same time."

Then who better to play in a story that could have been cowritten by the Marx Brothers and Dr. Elisabeth Kübler-Ross? When Harold Ramis first read Danny Rubin's original script for *Groundhog Day* (1993), he didn't laugh once...but he liked its spiri-

ABOVE: Dr. Leo Marvin (Richard Dreyfuss) and patient Bob Wiley (Bill Murray) in the delightfully dysfunctional What About Bob? (1991). RIGHT: Irritating anchorman Phil Connors (Bill Murray) and his acerbic cameraman Andy (Chris Elliot) celebrate Groundhog Day (1993). OPPOSITE: Director Harold Ramis gives notes to Murray and Andie MacDowell in Gobbler's Knob for Groundhog Day.

tuality and set to work. It follows a conceited, shallow, highly irritating Pittsburgh weatherman named Phil Connors (Bill Murray) to the chilly corner of Punxsutawney, Pennsylvania, to cover a groundhog (Punxsutawney Phil) who comes out each year on this day to see his shadow and foretell the coming of spring. Phil is accompanied by his producer, the sweet antithesis to his misanthropic personality, Rita (Andie MacDowell), and a cameraman, Andy (Chris Elliot), who knows Phil all too well.

After arriving the night before and resentfully covering the festivities at Gobbler's Knob for another year, Phil is ready to pack it in when a snowstorm—one he hasn't predicted—traps the trio for the night. A night in purgatory? No, but the next morning is, for when Phil's radio alarm clock hits 6:00 A.M. (to the annoying tune of Sonny and Cher's "I Got You, Babe"), it's Groundhog Day all over again...literally. Phil has become condemned to relive one day for the rest of eternity.

To say that Murray milks this surreally frustrating situation for every drop of comedy is an understatement. He had already made an unappreciated attempt at tackling life's tougher questions in the 1984 adaptation of William Somerset Maugham's *The Razor's Edge*. He wasn't going to be serious about it this time. The high energy of crown clown princes such as Robin Williams, Michael Keaton, Steve Martin, and even Billy Crystal would have driven audiences from their seats, but Murray's detached glibness makes his journey through this spiritual insanity a delight to watch. As the day repeats, Connors is disbelieving. The shrink he visits asks him to come back the next day. (He also wonders why he couldn't have been condemned endlessly to relive that day on vacation in Mexico, where he met a beautiful woman with whom he drank piña coladas, ate lobster, and made love on the beach "like frenzied sea otters.") He experiences freedom. He eats junk food like there's no tomorrow. He pumps a local beauty for information so that the next day—the same day— he can con her into bed. He robs an armored truck. He indulges in his adolescent fantasies and a high-speed police chase. He falls in love with Rita and misuses his new powers.

> Bill taught us that there was a magical, very American bliss to be achieved by failing in public and not realizing it.
> —Richard Corliss, *Time* magazine

He becomes an alcoholic. He attempts a stunning array of suicides. He tries to take the groundhog with him. He thinks he's God. And only then does he finally start to deal with his predicament: "What would you do if you only had one day to live?"

How anyone can be so grossly self-centered, so immorally flip, and yet so lovable and moving is a question we may never be able to answer. How Murray and Ramis like working together after six films is easier to respond to: "He harbors this grudging respect for my taste and judgment, if not my imagination," Ramis said. Ramis' judgment to use a montage of Murray getting his face slapped about a hundred times by an incensed MacDowell may have deep-ened that grudge. "He would say, 'Come on, Andie, really hit me,' and she would," re-called Ramis. "By the final take, his face was really swollen." Murray dryly added this about his costar: "Some people went to the Actor's Studio, some people came from Second City, she came out of some sort of wrestling college."

Face slaps weren't the only hazard. When Connors steals Punxsutawney Phil from the town mayor

> **Bill's persona sort of embodies the best and the worst in people. And I've lived with the voice of Bill Murray in my head for so long, it was kind of fun to think of him stuck in Punxsutawney and imag-ine the different ways he would approach Groundhog Day as he relived it over and over again.**
> **—Harold Ramis**

(Bill's brother, Brian Doyle Murray), he really has his hands full. The twenty-one-pound (9.5kg) groundhog, Scooter, had a propensity for biting, compelling the nervous Murray to blurt out such gems as "Don't drive angry" and "Not bad for a quadruped" as the snarling rodent, perched on the star's lap, gripped the wheel with his little claws. Of course, Scooter did eventually bite him three times during filming. The philosophical Murray only had this to say: "A costar that bites you once, well, I can accept that. A costar that bites you twice, now, that's a problem." What else could we expect from a man who has lived each day as his last, even if it were Groundhog Day?

A Childhood Memory

Let's face it, kids are funny. Although there are enough saccharine, cavorting, twisted tots out there in television and film land to make us cringe, a few have managed to make us drop all adult defenses and laugh ourselves silly.

Chaplin struck gold when he enlisted the support of cute little Jackie Coogan (later, ugly large Uncle Fester on television's *The Addams Family*) as *The Kid* (1920). Soon, every studio had its child stars, from Shirley Temple to Freddy Bartholomew. Hal Roach

Studios was even wiser to the comedic magic of children when Roach crafted one of the coolest comedy film series ever, *Our Gang*, which spawned the TV series *The Little Rascals*. Who didn't get a chuckle out of Spanky McFarland, Buckwheat, Fat Joe Cobb, Farina, and the rest of the gang? Who could forget their lilting musical theme, their kidlike contraptions, Darla Hood's reaction to the He-Man Woman-Haters Club, or Alfalfa's attempts at singing? Obviously not Hollywood, or they wouldn't have made a feature remake.

Comic screen depictions of childhood where the alleged child has acted like a real child, warts and all, have until recently been a rare commodity. Thanks to filmmaker François Truffaut, Jean-Pierre Léaud was able to mesmerize us as Antoine Doinelle in the classic French comedy *The 400 Blows* (1959). Tatum O'Neal's lonely little brat scored an Oscar for Best Supporting Actress in Peter Bogdanovich's black-and-white father-and-daughter story, *Paper Moon* (1973). And Jodie Foster launched her substantial career with

her androgynously seedy tomboy in Martin Scorsese's *Alice Doesn't Live Here Anymore* (1974).

In the past several years, great comedic turns by children have abounded, but usually as supporting players. Whitni Bright was tyrannically terrific as the temperamental daughter of unemployed actor Nick Nolte, who becomes a child star in *I'll Do Anything* (1994). Christina Ricci was as funny as she was unnerving as Wednesday

RIGHT: A growing boy needs milk, and sometimes he steals it if he's Jean-Pierre Léaud in François Truffaut's homage to youth, The 400 Blows (1959). BELOW: Whose heart haven't they stolen? Hal Roach's brainstorm brood of child actors were as cute as they came in the Our Gang films.

in *The Addams Family* (1991). As Arty and Eddie, Mike Damus and Jack Laufer bantered like a couple of seasoned vaudevillians while they were moving in with their grandmother in *Lost in Yonkers* (1993). At the top of this heap, one eleven-year-old Swedish actor, Anton Glanzelius, took the cake in a small film whose press release called it "a movie for everyone who ever thought their childhood was confusing": *My Life as a Dog* (1987).

The film's director, Lasse Hallstrom, had a childhood that was far from confusing. He had made his first film, a ten-minute thriller called *The Ghost Thief*, by the time he was ten years old. In high school, he started his professional career by making a 16-millimeter film of a local band and selling it to Swedish television. Films about childhood were a natural for the adult comedy director. With the help of Brasse Brannstrom and Per Berglund, he adapted Reidar Jonsson's tragicomic autobiographical novel into its big-screen version.

My Life as a Dog begins with a golden moment for its protagonist, Ingemar (Anton Glanzelius). He is on the beach with his charismatic mother (Anki Liden), making her howl with laughter with his funny stories and by clowning around on a driftwood crutch. The trouble is, that's just a memory. Ingemar is, in reality, barricaded at night inside his eccentric uncle's snowbound summerhouse (the one he built on someone else's property). The puckish-faced boy has just about come to the end of his tether from all the change and heartbreak that life has dealt him during the past year. The only way he can keep his sanity is by comparing his situation with those of people who are worse off, as he stares into the frosty heavens. He reminds himself of the Soviet space dog, Laika, who was sent into orbit for seven months without quite enough dog

food. There was the fellow who was impaled with a javelin while crossing a playing field. There was the missionary in Ethiopia who was beaten to death with clubs while teaching. There was the guy who watched a Tarzan movie and tried his swing out on a high tension wire. "You have to compare all the time," Ingemar narrates, "to get a distance on things."

Ingemar himself has come quite a distance. Life at home was less than idyllic. His father had abandoned him, running off to load bananas somewhere near the equator. The eccentric kid couldn't take a drink of milk without throwing it in his own face. His older brother caused all kinds of trouble, from getting Ingemar's penis stuck in a Coke bottle during a neighborhood sex-ed demonstration to making Ingemar soil his pajamas by waking him in the morning with an air rifle in the face. Their fiery-tempered mother, afflicted with tuberculosis, just didn't have the strength to deal with them.

After Ingemar fled the irate father of his sensible little girlfriend, who was caught undressing for him in their little playhouse underneath the railroad tracks, the boy decided to spare everyone a lot of trouble and live with his dog at the local dump. In an effort to keep them both warm, he burned the dump to the ground. So, it's goodbye to girlfriend, Mama, and his beloved dog, Sikan, and Ingemar is bundled off to live in the glassworks village of Smaland. There he enters a slow-paced, cozy, rural world of people who are even weirder than he is. He meets his soccer-coaching uncle Gunnar (Thomas von Bromssen), whose obsession with playing the Swedish recording of "I've Got a Lovely Bunch of Coconuts" is driving his wife, Ulla (Kicki Rundgren), crazy. There's old Mr.

Ingemar (Anton Glanzelius) shares something no doubt off-color with his eccentric uncle (Thomas Von Bromssen) in front of their summerhouse in **My Life as a Dog** *(1987).*

shot any of the other scenes that he was talking about. What was there to tell?

Fame was no thrill, either. According to Glanzelius, "In the beginning, everybody recognized me from the movie. Many would even point at me with their whole arm outstretched and talk about me very loud. I would have to look at the ground. That was not fun." So, like some child actors before him, despite the Swedish Oscar he got for best actor (the youngest ever to claim it) and in spite of one critic's hailing him as "a new Jack Nicholson" (what?) and periodic calls for a sequel, Anton Glanzelius has other plans—childhood, for one. "Soccer is my number-one priority. I hope to be a pro player in Brazil someday. I really love to play, and I think I can be what I want to be. It will be a natural for me." Does acting stand a chance? "If I suffered an injury and couldn't play, I might act in another movie."

The best never turn pro.

Arvidsson (Didrik Gustavsson) downstairs who covertly gets Ingemar to read to him out of women's underwear catalogs. There's Fransson (Magnus Rask), the nut across the street who spends his life working on his roof. There's Berit (Ingmari Carlsson), the voluptuous glassworker who wants Ingemar to chaperon her nude modeling for a famous sculptor (with shatteringly disastrous results). Last, there is Saga (Melinda Kinnaman), a girl incognito and the best athlete on his soccer team, who has her eyes on the new boy in town as her hormones start to rage.

Looking like a clean-cut, pint-size Michael J. Pollard, Glanzelius is so quirkily honest and so engaging as the hapless Ingemar that you're liable to head straight from the theater to the nearest Swedish adoption agency. Hallstrom saw the extraordinary young actor on Swedish television when the boy was only eight, and though the script called for an older Ingemar, the boy's audition left the director with "goose flesh"—and sent him to do a frantic rewrite of the role. For his own part, Glanzelius (who claimed, "Acting is not hard for me. I just play myself") "got to be close friends with the dog in the movie" and kept the twenty-person crew entertained with his impressions of Swedish pop stars, sometimes climbing a ladder to belt out his rendition of "Sweden Is Fantastic."

The youngster was less enthused about acting, however. The scenes where he throws his milk into his face took thirty soaking takes. The first shot, in which he tells his hospitalized mother of his new life, didn't make sense to Glanzelius because he hadn't yet

A Dark, Bright New Day for Comedy

Who said funny had to be nice? Who said every comedy had to be warm and fuzzy like *Sleepless in Seattle* (1993)? Who said one film genre (like comedies) had to steer clear of another (like thrillers)? It certainly wasn't Quentin Tarantino. In 1994, he rocked the moviegoing world with a film so dark, so violent, and so nonlinear that many thought it had absolutely no business being so light-hearted, so funny, and so thoughtful. *Pulp Fiction* is, of course, what we're talking here.

We're talking Vincent (a heroin-shooting John Travolta) and Jules (a Bible-quoting Samuel Jackson), two hit men for a drug lord named Marcellus Wallace (Ving Rhames) who have philosophical discussions about everything from the sexual ethics of foot massage to fast food in Amsterdam—just before they kill people. Mrs. Mia Wallace (Uma Thurman) is a lithe and charming cocaine addict who likes to enter dance competitions, especially when chaperoned by Vincent while her husband is away. However, bad things happen.

Butch (Bruce Willis) is a prizefighter being paid to take a fall by Marcellus, but he has other ideas, which have something to do with the wristwatch that his father hid for him in a Vietnamese concentration camp. (You guess where.) These ideas make him like to take big chances. His pixieish waif of a French girlfriend, Fabian (Mari De Medeiros), doesn't like it when he imitates a retarded person. A couple of urban *Deliverance*-type rednecks, Zed (Peter Greene) and Maynard (Duane Whitaker), like him a little too much. Really bad things happen when this plot intersects with the one before it.

Sunday-brunching, father figure Mr. Wolf (Harvey Keitel) is very helpful when it comes to cleaning up messes (like spattered brains) and solving problems (like a dead body missing those brains) in Jimmy's (Quentin Tarantino's) suburban home. Smack dealer Lance (Eric Stoltz) and his multipierced girlfriend, Jodie (Rosanna Arquette), aren't very helpful when it comes to reviving drug overdosers. Pumpkin (Tim Roth) and Honey Bunny (Amanda Plummer) are two diner robbers just helping themselves...until they bump into Jules and Vincent. Such incredibly bad (yet good) things happen.

Are these surreal film-noir types causing a little confusion? Well, when their stories are interwoven into a nontemporal but unstoppable chain of events to a pulsating retro-rock beat, and enriched with dialogue so organic that, in the words of producer Lawrence Bender, "you can chew it, eat it, and digest it," your confusion will end, and your laughter and screaming will begin.

Quentin Tarantino was a thirty-one-year-old former junior high school truant and ex-video-store jockey who had never even audited a film school class when he started to write movies. Luckily, his mom raised him right...on a lot of seventies flicks. The combination of laughs and terror appealed to him early: "The first movie I saw on television when I was, like, 'Oh wow, can you do this in a movie?' was *Abbott and Costello Meet Frankenstein*. That was my favorite movie when I was five years old. The Abbott and Costello stuff was funny, but when they went out of the room and the monsters would come on, they'd kill people!" He also liked the way that characters in the novels of J.D. Salinger and Larry McMurtry tended to float in and out of the story. With these eclectic aesthetics, he went to work on the script for his first film, the small-time hoodfest *Reservoir Dogs* (1992).

> *Along the way, people are riddled with bullets, a victim's brains are spattered like pureed mango all over the inside of a car, a drug-overdosed woman has a 6-inch [15.2cm] hypodermic needle rammed into her heart, a man is tied up and sodomized. All in good fun, Tarantino style.*
> **—Jack Matthews in Newsweek, on Pulp Fiction (1994)**

As yet unknown, but a persuasive and marathon talker, Tarantino convinced Harvey Keitel into heading up the $24,000-budgeted flick, and on the strength of the star's participation, Tarantino managed to jack the budget up to $400,000. It was a cult smash. His bloodily funny *True Romance* (1993) script and his follow-up psychopathic stab at the media, *Natural Born Killers* (1994), sold like hotcakes. Next, inspired by the *Black Mask* crime magazines of yesteryear, he collided past with the present in a viciously funny story of spiritual redemption—and the blood and other by-products you have to wade through to get it. This was gonna be a different kind of comedy, for, as Tarantino said,

> *It's not like I'm on a crusade against linear narrative. What I am against is saying it's the only game in town.*
> **—Quentin Tarantino, filmmaker and iconoclast**

"I don't think there's any such thing as 'too funny' or that there's any such thing as 'too hard.' But I don't do it like *Abbott and Costello Meet Frankenstein*, where you're at the funny part, then you're at the scary part, then you're at the funny part again. To me, all my stuff is the funny part."

One of those funny parts, the infamous needle scene, sent a viewer into insulin shock at *Pulp Fiction*'s New York Film Festival premiere, stopping the proceedings for nine minutes. When Samuel Jackson read the script, he went into another kind of shock: "I couldn't believe it. I sat down to read it and immediately, when I finished, went back to the front to read it again and make sure I'd read what I'd read, because I'd never read a script that good—and I've read a lot of scripts."

Bad boys and don't they know it—Quentin Tarantino (left) and cowriter Roger Avary off the set of Pulp Fiction (1994).

ABOVE: *Harvey Keitel (right) and Steve Buscemi see who's top dog in* Reservoir Dogs *(1992).* BELOW, LEFT AND RIGHT: *Having fun at Jack Rabbit Slim's, Vincent (John Travolta) is caught mid-frug and Mia (Uma Thurman) mid-shake in* Pulp Fiction.

Where else can you find a gangster quoting Ezekiel, or planning to put his rod down and "walk the earth, like Cain in *Kung Fu*"? The everyday details that almost all the characters deal with as they live their dangerous and high-stakes lives are key to this wild ride, as were Tarantino and cowriter Roger Avary's (Avary wrote the Butch storyline) complete unwillingness to be predictable. "Let's say you're being chased by the cops," poses Tarantino, "and you yank somebody out of their car to get away, but maybe their seatbelt gets stuck, or maybe they drive a stick and you don't drive a stick. It's those messy little things that are actually funny. Movies have a ten-

dency to build up to a moment and then boom, you cut. I wanted to stay in that moment. I love not making it easy by cutting."

But *Pulp Fiction* wouldn't have sent audiences home laughing, nerve-wracked, or in an ambulance if he hadn't hired the cast that he did. While writing the script, Tarantino had invited has-been superstar John Travolta over to his house for a marathon chat. They talked for twelve hours. They drank wine. They went out to dinner. They came home and played around with Quentin's *Welcome Back Kotter, Grease,* and *Saturday Night Fever* board games and admired his lunchbox collection. Nary a word was said about the project. Then, in Travolta's words, "Quentin let me have it. He said, 'What did you do? Don't you remember what Pauline Kael said about you? What Truffaut said about you? Do you know what you mean to the American cinema? John, what did you do?'" The words both chastened Travolta and renewed his sense of worth. Tarantino tailored the role of Vincent for the errant acting icon, and after worrying a little about the role model that his role might project, Travolta dived in and started hanging out with junkies to get the mind-set. On the set, he claims that Tarantino "lets you put all the icing on the cake. For Vincent, I could mock up the hair, the accent, the walk, the talk." Uma Thurman agrees that, for someone with a definite vision, Tarantino lets his actors collaborate the way few directors have the courage to. "I like the idea that all these characters could be the star of their own movie," Tarantino boasts, "and as far as they're concerned, when they come in, they are."

SOME THINGS NEVER CHANGE

Boys will be boys. Comedy has matured, but let's not go so far as to say that it's mature. Guys still write a lot of it, and a lot of it reflects the male psyche...a little too accurately. Before you grow up and close the book, see if you can tag these libidinal lines with the mouths of the overgrown infants, boys, and adolescents who made them famous. We've even thrown in a woman, to keep you guessing.

A) "My mama always said life is like a box of choco-lates."

B) "I know I'm God because whenever I pray, I find I'm talking to myself."

C) "I know you are, but what am I?"

D) "The only reason you're still living is because I never kissed you."

E) "Bring a pitcher of beer every seven minutes until someone passes out, then bring one every ten minutes."

F) "If this is foreplay, I'm a dead man."

G) "That's not a knife....That's a knife."

H) "I'll be takin' these Huggies and...uh, whatever cash you've got."

I) "Feed me, Seymour....Feed me all night long."

J) "I'm not bad, I'm just drawn that way."

K) "Joey, have you ever been in a Turkish prison?"

L) "K-Mart sucks!"

M) "I think I'll take a bath." "I'll alert the media."

N) "I'm a zit, get it?"

O) "They was giving me 10,000 watts a day, and you know, I'm hot to trot. The next woman who takes me out is going to light up like a pinball machine and pay off in silver dollars."

P) "Pardon me, boy. Is this the Transylvania station?"

Q) "I don't tan—I stroke."

R) "I told you 158 times, I cannot stand little notes on my pillow. 'We're out of corn flakes. F.U.' It took me three hours to figure out F.U. was Felix Ungar. It's not your fault, Felix; it's a rotten combination, that's all."

S) "This is your neighbor speaking. I'm sure I speak for all of us when I say that something must be done about your garbage cans in the alley here. It is definitely sec-ond-rate garbage! Now, by next week I want to see a better class of garbage. I want to see champagne bot-tles and caviar cans. I'm sure you're all behind me on this, so let's snap it up and get on the ball!"

T) "I'm a woman!" "Well, nobody's perfect."

U) "We came, we saw, we kicked ass."

V) "This is the screwiest picture I was ever in."

Answers: A) *Tom Hanks in Forrest Gump* (1994), B) *Peter O'Toole in The Ruling Class* (1971), C) *Pee-Wee Herman in Pee-Wee's Big Adventure* (1985), D) *Charles Durning in Tootsie* (1982), E) *Rodney Dangerfield in Back to School* (1986), F) *Steve Guttenberg in Cocoon* (1985), G) *Paul Hogan in Crocodile Dundee* (1986), H) *Nicolas Cage in Raising Arizona* (1987), I) *The Plant in Little Shop of Horrors* (1986), J) *Kathleen Turner as Jessica Rabbit in Who Framed Roger Rabbit?* (1988), K) *Peter Graves in Airplane* (1980), L) *Dustin Hoffman in Rain Man* (1988), M) *Dudley Moore and Sir John Gielgud in Arthur* (1981), N) *John Belushi in Animal House* (1978), O) *Jack Nicholson in One Flew Over the Cuckoo's Nest* (1975), P) *Gene Wilder in Young Frankenstein* (1974), Q) *Woody Allen in Play It Again, Sam* (1972), R) *Walter Matthau in The Odd Couple* (1968), S) *Jason Robards, Jr., in A Thousand Clowns* (1965), T) *Jack Lemmon and Joe E. Brown in Some Like It Hot* (1959), U) *Bill Murray in Ghostbusters* (1984), V) *The Camel in Road to Morocco* (1942)

They were. Five Academy awards and a Cannes Film Festival Palm D'Or later, Pulp Fiction, with its nastiness, vio-lence, and a plot that doubles and redoubles back on itself, has become an iconoclastic retro-refit inspiration for filmmakers everywhere. The style wheel has come full circle, and what was old is suddenly very new—and juiced to the max. Does this mean that classics of the future will have a middle, a beginning, and then an end? Will slapstick situations need bleach to remove the bloodstains? Maybe not, but as the laughs and the end of the mil-lennium come rolling in, comedy should be about as stable, undisputed, and predictable as this cuddly world we live in. Brace yourself!

Bibliography

Abbott and Costello Meet Jerry Seinfeld. NBC Television.

Adamson, Joe. *Groucho, Harpo, Chico, and Sometimes Zeppo*. New York: Simon & Schuster, 1973.

Adler, Jerry, and Roy Sawhill. "Every Groundhog Has His Day." *Newsweek*, March 8, 1993.

All of Me. Press kit. Universal Studios.

Amis, Martin. "Travolta's Second Act." *New Yorker*, February 20, 1995.

Anobile, Richard J. *A Flask of Fields*. New York: Darien House, 1972.

"Anton Glanzelius Unleashes a Fierce Talent in 'My Life as a Dog.' " *People*, August 10, 1987.

Arquette, Rosanna. "Look Who's Talking." *Interview*, August 1994.

"At the Movies." *New York Times*, October 12, 1984.

Barthel, Joan. "Mel Brooks: To Lie and Sound Jolly?" *New York Times*, September 3, 1967.

"Bedazzled." *Variety*, December 13, 1967.

Bergan, Ronald. *The Life and Times of the Marx Brothers*. New York: Smithmark, 1992.

Bjorkmat, Stig. *Woody Allen on Woody Allen*. New York: Grove Press, 1993.

"Boo!" *New Yorker*, April 18, 1988.

Brodie, John. "The Tail That Wails the Dog." *Gentlemen's Quarterly*, August 1994.

Brown, Jared. *Zero Mostel*. New York: Atheneum, 1989.

Brownlow, Kevin. *The Parade's Gone By*. New York: Knopf, 1968.

Bull, Peter. "The Ending You Never Saw in 'Strangelove.' " *New York Times*, January 9, 1966.

Byrge, Duane, and Robert Milton Miller. *The Screwball Comedy Films*. Jefferson, N.C.: McFarland, 1991.

Canby, Vincent. "Buster Keaton's Five-Star General." *New York Times*, August 1, 1971.

Capra, Frank. *The Name Above the Title*. New York: Macmillan, 1971.

Champlin, Charles. "Allen Awakens Silent Comedy in 'Sleeper.' " *Los Angeles Times*, December 23, 1973.

Cheshire, Godfrey. "Hollywood's New Hit Men." *Interview*, September 1994.

Christagau, Robert, and Carola Dibbell. "The Men in the Band." *Village Voice*, March 6, 1984.

Cohen, Joan L. *The Awful Truth*—program notes. The Los Angeles County Museum of Art, August 7, 1976.

Colombo, Robert. *Popcorn in Paradise: The Wit and Wisdom of Hollywood*. New York: Holt, Rinehart, and Winston, 1980.

Corliss, Richard. "Bill Murray in the Driver's Seat." *Time*, March 8, 1993.

———."A Blast to the Heart." *Time*, October 10, 1994.

Crisafulli, Chuck. "It's Zany and Aces with Fans." *Los Angeles Times*, February 18, 1994.

Curtis, James. *Between Flops: A Biography of Preston Sturges*. New York: Harcourt Brace Jovanovich, 1982.

Daly, Phil M. "Along the Male." *Film Daily*, March 9, 1963.

Dardis, Tom. *Keaton: The Man Who Wouldn't Lie Down*. New York: Charles Scribner and Sons, 1979.

D'Arne, Wilson. "One Man Movie Factory." *Picturegoer Weekly Literary Digest*, November 2, 1935.

Descaner, Donald. "Bringing Up Baby—The R.K.O. Years"—program notes. The Los Angeles County Museum of Art, August 3, 1977.

Duck Soup—Film Circle program. University of Wisconsin, August 11, 1964.

Duck Soup—program notes. The Franklin Institute, April 1957.

Duncan-Shannon, Jody. "For Your Consideration: The Effects of Beetlejuice." *Cinefex*, May 1988.

Edelstein, David. "Mixing Beetlejuice." *Rolling Stone*, June 2, 1988.

Epstein, Jerry. *Remembering Charlie: A Pictorial Biography*. New York: Doubleday, 1989.

Epstein, Robert. "Forrest Gump's Proud Dad." *Los Angeles Times*, August 7, 1994.

Evans, Harry. "Charlie's Latest." *Family Circle*, March 2, 1936.

Everson, William K. *The Art of W.C. Fields*. New York: Bonanza Books, 1967.

Falk, Quentin. "Brian—An Epic in the Making." *Screen International*, November 10, 1979.

Fields, Ronald J. *W.C. Fields: A Life on Film*. New York: St. Martin's Press, 1984.

Franklin, Joe. *Joe Franklin's Encyclopedia of Comedians*. Secaucus, N.J.: Citadel Press, 1979.

Frederick, Robert B. "Education of Bright, Young: Gotta Have Experienced Producers; How 'Bedazzled' Shed Distractions." *Variety*, December 13, 1967.

Furmanek, Bob, and Ron Palumbo. *Abbott and Costello in Hollywood*. New York: Perigee Books, 1991.

Gable, Clark. "The Role I Liked Best." *The Saturday Evening Post*, May 17, 1947.

Gambaccini, Paul. "The Persecution of Monty Python's 'Life of Brian.' " *Rolling Stone*, October 18, 1979.

Gehring, Wes D. *Screwball Comedy: A Genre of Madcap Romance*. New York: Greenwood Press, 1986.

"Ghostly Experience." *Long Beach* (Calif.) *Press Telegram*, June 13, 1987.

Giles, Jeff. "Funny Face." *Newsweek*, June 25, 1995.

Gilliat, Penelope. *Jacques Tati*. London: Woburn House, 1976.

The Gods Must Be Crazy—production notes. Twentieth Century Fox and T.L.C. Films.

Gold, Ronald. "Producers: Fantasy of 'Creation.' " *Variety*, May 10, 1967.

Grant, Lee. "Care, Feeding of 'S.O.B.'—'High Style' or 'Fat'?" *Los Angeles Times*, June 25, 1981.

Groundhog Day. Press kit. Columbia Pictures.

Harmetz, Aljean. "Book by Kosinski, Film by Ashby." *New York Times*, December 22, 1979.

Harvey, James. *Romantic Comedy*. New York: Knopf, 1987.

Heise, Jeff. "Program Note—Odd Man in a Tribute to Peter Sellers." *American Cinematheque*, April 11, 1993.

Herman, Gary. *The Book of Hollywood Quotes*. New York: Omnibus Press, 1979.

Higgins, John. "The Sleeper That Took Off." *London Times*, April 27, 1974.

Hind, John. "Cook Tease." *Time Out*, January 30, 1991.

Hoberman, J. "Livin' Large." *Village Voice*, September 13, 1994.

"Is the State Department Out to Muzzle 'Dr. Strangelove'?" *Variety*, February 25, 1964.

"It's Not Quite 'Remains of the Day.' " *Newsweek*, February 21, 1994.

Kendall, Elizabeth. *The Runaway Bride*. New York: Knopf, 1990.

Kennedy, Lisa. "Natural Born Filmmaker: Quentin Tarantino Versus the Film Geeks." *Village Voice*, October 25, 1994.

Kerr, Walter. *The Silent Clowns*. New York: Knopf, 1975.

Kilday, Gregg. "Blake Edwards on the Battlements." *Los Angeles Herald Examiner*, June 29, 1981.

Kirkpatrick, Curry. "Tales of Celebrity Babylon." *Newsweek*, June 27, 1994.

Kroll, Jack. "Whose Body Is It, Anyway?" *Newsweek*, September 17, 1984.

Lahr, John. "Bedazzled." *New Yorker*, January 23, 1975.

Langman, Larry. *Encyclopedia of American Film Comedy*. New York: Garland Publishing, 1987.

Lax, Eric. *On Being Funny: Woody Allen and Comedy*. New York: Charter House, 1975.

———. *Woody Allen: A Biography*. New York: Knopf, 1991.

Lefkowitz, Eric. "'Dr. Strangelove' Turns 30: Can It Still Be Trusted?" *New York Times*, January 30, 1994.

Lieberman, Jane. "Short Brings 'Simple' Approach to Complex SFX Work." *Variety*, April 29, 1988.

"Lily Tomlin Gets Inside Steve Martin." *Rolling Stone*, December 8, 1983.

Malachosky, Tim, and James Greene. *Mae West*. San Diego: Empire Publishing, 1993.

Maugh, Thomas H. "Researchers Attempt to Pinpoint Alien Hand Syndrome." *Los Angeles Times*, April 25, 1991.

McBride, Joseph. *Hawks on Hawks*. Los Angeles: University of California Press, 1982.

McCabe, John, and Al Kilgore. *Laurel and Hardy*. New York: E.P. Dutton, 1975.

McGuigan, Kathleen, Donna Foote, and Jennifer Schenker. "Not Just Child's Play." *Newsweek*, February, 22, 1988.

———. "A Spinal Tap for Your Health." *Newsweek*, May 14, 1984.

Meisel, Myron. "Blake Edwards Tells His S.O.B. Stories." *Los Angeles Reader*, July 3, 1981.

Mills, Nancy. "All of Me." *Marquee*, August-September 1984.

Obalil, Linda. *Duck Soup*—program notes. *Cinema Texas*, vol. 13, no. 4 (January 19, 1978).

———. *The General*—program notes. *Cinema Texas*, vol. 14, no. 1 (February 7, 1978).

"One Man's Movie." *Saturday Review*, June 19, 1954.

Peoples, Sam. "Mad Cap." *Classic Film Collector*, winter 1970.

"Peter Sellers Kills Three Roles in Kubrick Film." *Greater Amusements*, February 14, 1964.

Potterton, Reg. "The Gospel According to Monty Python." *Playboy*, November 19, 1979.

"The Producers." *Time*, January 26, 1968.

"Resouled." *Playboy*, April 1984.

Ringnalda, Margaret B. "Danger! Genius at Work!" *Screenland*, October 1935.

Robertson, Patrick. *Guinness Film Facts and Feats*. London: Guinness Books, 1985.

Rodler, Leslie. *Monsieur Hulot's Holiday*—program notes. *Cinema Texas*, vol. 26, no. 3 (March 19, 1984).

Rosenbaum, Ralph. "Evil's Back." *New York Times Sunday Magazine*, June 14, 1995.

Rosenblum, Ralph, and Robert Karen. "The Making of *Annie Hall*." *New York Magazine*, October 8, 1979.

Sanders, Richard. "Monty Python's 'Life of Brian' Is Raising Holy Hell." *Us* magazine, October 16, 1979.

Sarris, Andrew. "The Travails of Tati, the God Children of Goddard." *Village Voice*, November 17, 1983.

Scagnetti, Jack. *The Laurel and Hardy Scrapbook*. Middle Village, N.Y.: Jonathan David Publishers, 1976.

Schever, Philip K. "Kubrick Explains Movie of Absurd." *Los Angeles Times*, May 21, 1963.

Schickel, Richard. "Biting the Hand of Hollywood." *Time*, July 13, 1981.

———. *Harold Lloyd: The Shape of Laughter*. Boston: New York Graphic Society, 1974.

Schoenberger, Nancy. *A Talent for Genius: The Life and Times of Oscar Levant*. New York: Villard Books, 1994.

Shepard, Dick. "The Oh-So-Sad Saga of 'Bad Luck' Mabel Normand." *Los Angeles Herald Examiner*, June 30, 1982.

Skretvedt, Randy. *Laurel and Hardy: The Magic Behind the Movies*. Beverly Hills, Calif.: Moonstone Press, 1987.

Spector, Warren. *Annie Hall*—program notes. *Cinema Texas*, vol. 19, no. 1 (September 4, 1980).

Spignesi, Stephen J. *The Woody Allen Companion*. Kansas City: Andrews and McMeel, 1992.

Starr, Michael. *Peter Sellers: A Film History*. Jefferson, N.C.: McFarland, 1991.

Stern, Daniel. "Candide of the Electronic Age." *Life*, April 30, 1971.

Strick, Philip. Great Films of the Century—no. 14: "The General." *Films and Filming*, September 1961.

Sweet, Jeff. "Beyond 'Beyond the Fringe.'" *Los Angeles Times*, December 27, 1973.

This Is Spinal Tap. Promotional materials, Embassy Pictures, 1984.

Thomas, Dan. "Charlie Chaplin Is at Work Again." *Film Pictorial*, December 22, 1934.

Thompson-George, Cathy. "Tom Hanks Shows His Gumption." *Entertainment Today*, July 1, 1994.

Tyler, Parker. *Chaplin: Last of the Clowns*. New York: Horizon Press, 1972.

Walker, Alexander. *Peter Sellers: The Authorized Biography*. New York: Macmillan, 1981.

Watt, Michael. "Monty Python on the Trail Chasing the Elusive Messiah." *Los Angeles Times*, December 31, 1978.

Weinstein, Steve. "Happily Living on the Cranky Comic Edge." *Los Angeles Times*, February 22, 1993.

Weintraub, Ed. *The Wit and Wisdom of Mae West*. New York: G.B. Putnam and Sons, 1967.

"We Never Promised You a Rose Garden." *Los Angeles Herald Examiner*, January 22, 1980.

Wilde, Larry. *The Great Comedians Talk About Comedy*. New York: Citadel Press, 1968.

Williams, Clem. "Comic Mayhem: The Films of Preston Sturges." The Los Angeles County Museum of Art, October 8, 1982.

Willman, Chris. "Reality Check." *Los Angeles Times*, March 22, 1992.

Winokur, Jon. *True Confessions*. New York: Dutton Books, 1982.

Wolf, Leslie. "The Splendors of Stupidity: *This Is Spinal Tap*." *L.A. Weekly*, April 27, 1984.

Young, Robert, Jr. *Roscoe Fatty Arbuckle: A Bio-Bibliography*. Westport, Conn.: Greenwood Press, 1994.

Photography Credits

All photography from The Kobal Collection except:

Archive Photos: pp. 10–11, 12 top, 14 left, 17, 21, 22 top, 28–29, 30, 34, 35 both, 42

Corbis-Bettmann Archive: pp. 13, 15, 88 top, 119 top

Photofest: pp. 66 top, 76 bottom, 89 bottom, 91, 96 top, 100, 101, 104–105, 111 bottom, 117 top

Springer/Corbis-Bettmann Film Archive: p. 37

UPI/Corbis-Bettmann: p. 8

Index